SPACES OF THE MIND

Martha Graham in Frontier, *1935.* © Barbara Morgan

SPACES OF THE MIND

Isamu Noguchi's Dance Designs

Robert Tracy

First Edition, November 2000

Copyright © 2001 by Robert Tracy.
Published by Proscenium Publishers, Inc., 118 East 130th Street, New York, NY 10016.
All rights reserved under International and Pan-American copyright conventions.

Cover and interior design by Bryan McHugh.

Library of Congress Cataloging-in-Publication Data

Tracy, Robert
    Spaces of the mind: Isamu Noguchi's dance designs / Robert Tracy.—1st Limelight ed.
        p cm.
    ISBN 0-87910-952-1—ISBN 0-87910-953-X (pbk.)
        1. Noguchi, Isamu, 1904—Criticism and interpretation. 2. Dance—Stage-setting and scenery.
3. Martha Graham Dance Company. I. Noguchi, Isamu, 1904- II. Title.

NB237.N6 T73 2000
792.8'9025'092—dc21

                                                                    00-045120

Manufactured in the United States of America.

Spaces of the Mind *is dedicated to the memory of*

Isamu Noguchi

Lincoln Kirstein } *3 giant mentoring spirits*

Rudolf Nureyev

and

4 Mom—all of you everywhere

predominantly Helen and Berry

in my own personal odyssey

and

2 all my friends

past, present, future

for sharing infinite possibilities

on this space journey—

with deepest appreciation

to

Rosalie,

Andréa, Bob, Hinton, Judith, Rifat, Susan and James^2

"These are spaces of the mind that Martha is dealing with.
These are situations of birth and renewal—mysteries, you might say....
I suppose my contribution is a spatial division."

Isamu Noguchi

CONTRIBUTING PHOTOGRAPHERS

Arnold Eagle

and

Nan Melville

Carolyn George

Cris Alexander

Philippe Halsman

Barbara Morgan

Max Waldman

Rudolf Burckhardt

Anthony Crickmay

Johan Elbers

Fred Fehl

Jaacov Agor

Sam Frank

David Fullard

George Platt Lynes

Louis Peres

Martha Swope

Beatriz Schiller

Jack Vartoogian

CONTENTS

ISAMU NOGUCHI
ART AND DANCE

"Art is everywhere. The whole world is art. The only thing is, some people see it and some people don't," said sculptor Isamu Noguchi in 1987. "If one is really awake, he will see the whole world is a symphony you can actually hear and walk around in and observe all the different manifestations."

Isamu Noguchi was born in Los Angeles, California, on November 17, 1904. His parents, Leonie Gilmour, an American writer, and Yonejiro (Yone) Noguchi, a Japanese poet and scholar, met in New York in 1901. "Actually," Noguchi said, "my mother's name 'Gilmour' is a Scottish form. It was a Scottish family that had moved to Ulster and then they came to New York." Yone Noguchi deserted Gilmour before their son's birth and returned to Japan, where he had accepted a teaching position at the prestigious Keiō University. Gilmour traveled to the West Coast to be with her mother and sister during her pregnancy. In 1906, after a prolonged correspondence, the young boy and his mother joined Yone in Tokyo; by 1908, Isamu Noguchi's parents lived apart, and he saw less and less of his father. Gilmour and her son moved to the seaside: first to Omori in 1910, then to Chigasaki in 1912, the year Noguchi's sister, Ailes Gilmour, was born. Yone Noguchi married in 1913 and created a traditional Japanese family. Gilmour had become an editor of the *Far Eastern Review*.

Inspired by her own education at Bryn Mawr, Gilmour—who had sole responsibility for her son's upbringing—would read poems by William Blake, Chaucer's tales, and stories from Greek mythology to her son, thus planting the seeds which would influence him artistically and establishing the foundation of a prolific creative life. "You see, I was the product of an American woman's imagination," Noguchi later explained.

By the age of ten, Noguchi had learned how to use Japanese woodworking tools and was apprenticed to a Japanese woodcarver. Indeed, he had helped build the family's home in Chigasaki. He attended Japanese schools until 1916, when he was sent to St. Joseph's College, a Jesuit school in Yokohama. His mother and sister followed in 1917. In 1918, he was sent alone to America to attend the Interlacken School in Rolling Prairie, Indiana. He arrived with a bag of tools and began carving a frieze of seaweed, fish, and shells on his bedboard. Later in life Noguchi commented, "Man must leave his imprint too, because he is part of nature."

After the school was closed a few months later for use by the military, its founder, Dr. Edward Rumely, placed Noguchi with a Swedenborgian minister, Dr. Samuel Mack, in La Porte, Indiana. In 1922, Noguchi, who was known as "Sam Gilmour" at that time, graduated from La Porte High School and spent the following summer in Connecticut tutoring the son of sculptor Gutzon Borglum, the creator of Mount Rushmore, in exchange for sculpture lessons. Rumely raised funds for Noguchi to attend Columbia University, and in the fall, Noguchi moved to New York City to begin his premed studies. His mother, who had returned to California in 1923 and moved to New York

City in 1924, encouraged Noguchi to enroll in sculpture classes at the Leonardo da Vinci Art School while continuing his studies at Columbia.

Noguchi left Columbia in 1924. Later, he explained that he dropped the name "Gilmour" and assumed his father's surname "when I first decided I was going to be a sculptor. I was nineteen."

Two years later, Noguchi executed his first designs for dance, creating papier maché masks for Michio Ito, a Japanese interpretive dancer who was performing the Nōh theater-influenced play, *At the Hawk's Well*, by William Butler Yeats.

"Ito wanted to produce the drama here in New York," Noguchi said. "I think he knew Yeats in London. He knew a lot of people. He had a lot of credentials."

Also in 1926, Noguchi discovered the sculpture of the great, Romanian-born artist, Constantin Brancusi. Through a Guggenheim Fellowship, Noguchi moved to Paris where he became Brancusi's assistant for two years.

"Brancusi made me realize that what I had learned previously—the quick ways of doing things—was all wrong," he said. "I learned the tricks of the trade, after all. If you want to do academic things, you can do them that way. It is not difficult."

He continued, "The difficulty is really what we are talking about. It is the difficulty, the mistakes, and the dead ends from which artists develop. It is not the quick solutions. It is not something you learn and apply. After all, it is a search

you have to enter into yourself."

Later Noguchi would say, "Any person I've been influenced by, I've been obliged to betray."

In the late 1920s, Noguchi was occupied with carving portrait heads of influential members of society and artists, including George Gershwin, Buckminster Fuller, Lincoln Kirstein, Michio Ito, and Martha Graham. Noguchi's sister, Ailes Gilmour, was a member of the Martha Graham Group from 1930 to 1933. Noguchi's mother sewed costumes for Graham as well.

"I knew Martha very well," Noguchi recalled. "I did two heads of her in 1928, [during] that winter period when I had a studio on top of Carnegie Hall and she had a studio there, too. I used to see her quite often. Martha insisted I do the second head to be more as she wished. The first was too close to a reality which she aspired to rise above."

Noguchi returned to Paris in April 1930 and stayed for two months. He then traveled via Moscow to Beijing, where he spent seven months studying the art of Chinese brush paintings with master Ch'i Pai-shih. In March 1931, he arrived in Japan, where he became reacquainted with his father, Yone. Their reunion proved difficult—in fact, Yone Noguchi had warned his son not to arrive in Tokyo using the name "Noguchi." Of this time Noguchi said, "We had long and silent conversations. *Moyen de parle*. It's a way of talking after all, like Lincoln Kirstein said, that he got along very well with Balanchine because they never spoke to each other. That is what you call 'long and silent conversations.'"

3

Isamu Noguchi left in May and traveled to Kyoto, where he studied ancient pottery techniques and worked in Jinmatsu Unō's pottery. It was in Kyoto that Noguchi saw Haniwa sculptures[1] and Zen gardens. Said the sculptor, "That is when I had a real dose of garden making. My learning is not what one would call 'going to school.' I didn't want to be a Japanese gardener. I'm talking about a general osmosis. After all, it took me sixty years."

When Noguchi returned to New York City in October 1931, the first sculpture he created was a futuristic, Haniwa-inspired piece, named "Miss Expanding Universe" by Buckminster Fuller. Noguchi's first costume design for dance, executed in 1932, was for *The Expanding Universe,* a solo dance choreographed by good friend Ruth Page. The dress design was inspired by that sculpture.

In 1935, Noguchi was commissioned by Martha Graham to create a set for *Frontier,* Graham's romantic dance-drama based on the development of the American West, with music by Louis Horst. It was Noguchi's first set design for dance. Noguchi designed one more set for Graham—*Chronicle* (1936)—before their major collaboration began in the mid-1940s. Over the course of their collaboration, Noguchi produced fifteen sculptural set designs for dances which Graham based on Greek mythology and biblical texts; ultimately Graham would choreograph twenty-five works danced in settings by Noguchi. Thus began what is arguably one of the most important collaborations in twentieth century dance theater.

"When the time came for me to work with larger spaces," said Noguchi, "I conceived them as gardens, not as sites with objects, but as relationships to a whole. I would say this came from my knowledge of the dance theater where there is evidently a totality of experience by the audience."

In the mid-Thirties, at the same time he was creating his socially-conscious sculptures, Noguchi traveled to Mexico City to carve a 72-foot long by 6-$\frac{1}{2}$-foot high mural depicting the history of the Mexican revolution, "History Mexico 1936," in the Indian market of Abelardo Rodriguez behind the cathedral. Interestingly, one year later, on April 26, 1937, the German air force, acting under the order of Francisco Franco, bombed and almost completely destroyed the Spanish city of Guernica, the most ancient town of the Basques and the center of their cultural tradition. Within days Pablo Picasso began work on his iconoclastic mural "Guernica," encapsulating the Spanish Civil War in oil on canvas. As Picasso stated, art is used not to decorate apartments but as an instrument of war against the enemy.

Social protest was prevalent when Noguchi returned to New York. He won a major commission for a relief sculpture to be situated over the entrance of the Associated Press building in Rockefeller Center. It was cast as a nine-ton stainless steel plaque and foretold of war. Shortly thereafter Noguchi realized his first fountain proposal, the Ford Fountain for the 1939 World's Fair, which has since been destroyed.

In the early Forties, Noguchi began creating

4

relief sculptures in the form of imaginary landscapes, and by 1944 he designed a table for the Herman Miller Company which related to his landscape sculptures. By the mid-Forties he had produced a series of interlocking sculptures; at the same time, he was drafting numerous unrealized visionary proposals, including a large earthwork sculpture to be seen from Mars (1947). About that work he said, "It's the only remaining record of my interest in making earth mounds such as those of the American Indian." In the late Forties Noguchi traveled throughout Europe, the Near East, India, Southeast Asia, and Japan, studying cathedrals, plazas, temples, monoliths, and monuments.

For sixty years Noguchi was able to create environmental expressions through his deep understanding of stone. Noguchi's geological landscapes and topographical landmarks included projects such as playgrounds, gardens, fountains, and parks. His first garden, "Readers Digest," and interior were realized at Keiō University in the early Fifties. Through the materials he employed, like aluminum, bronze, marble, metal, granite, wood, and paper, Noguchi was able to define his space. The impressive scope of Noguchi's artistic explorations was succinctly summed up by the artist himself:

> I came to realize all is sculpture, whether garden, theater or playground. All are part of the human context. It is a metaphor for my world, which is changing all the time. People put everything into categories. I don't go according to some

sort of schedule. People try to put everything into schedules, categories. . . . And critics just don't interest me. It's foreign to my way of thinking. But art is extensive on many levels, not only on a visual level.

In fact, his furniture and lamp designs, particularly the *Akari*, or light sculptures, dating from the 1940s, are still available and in vogue to this day. Noguchi continued to explore the use of different media throughout his career: In the early 1950s, he exhibited ceramics; he was working on cast-iron pieces in Japan and executing sculptures in Greek marble in the mid-1950s; by the late 1950s, he was working with sheet metal. In 1966 he exhibited floor sculptures and multi-part bronzes. From 1967 to 1970, Noguchi worked on stone and metal sculptures. In addition, Noguchi's brush drawings were shown concurrently with his 1968 retrospective at the Whitney Museum, and he created the fountains for Expo '70 held in Osaka, Japan.

Martin Friedman, who curated "Noguchi's Imaginary Landscapes," a major 1978 retrospective of the sculptor's designs at the Walker Art Center in Minneapolis, wrote,

> Noguchi came to artistic maturity in the 1940s, when infatuation with the unconscious and the dream world inspired a generation of Surrealist artists to adventure in the hallucinatory landscape of the mind. Erotic and demonic entities inhab-

ited his terrain, constantly varying their aspects to express a range of human emotion and elemental experiences—birth, love, anguish, jealousy, death. Analogies between universal myths and modern day behavior posited by Freud and Jung exerted powerful appeal for American artists.

Of the sixteen designs for dance which Noguchi created during the Forties, twelve were for the Martha Graham Company, and although Graham and Noguchi generally approached the creation of their works from different points of view, their collaborations expressed similar intentions and ultimately evoked timeless images of the majestic universal legends which Graham positioned from a woman's standpoint: Medea, Jocasta, Ariadne, Clytemnestra, Alcestis, Phaedra, Circe, Hecuba, Helen of Troy, the Virgin Mary, Hérodiade, Judith, and Joan of Arc. A unique language emerged out of the so-called Graham-Noguchi "mythological cycle," which communicated to the public on a new emotional and intellectual level and emphasized an understanding of space, rhythm, and kinetics. Noguchi's other dance collaborations included sets for choreographers George Balanchine, Merce Cunningham, Erick Hawkins, Yuriko Anemiya Kikuchi (known as "Yuriko"), Ruth Page and Kei Takei.

Noguchi's only set and costumes designs for a purely theatrical production were for the Royal Shakespeare Company's *King Lear*, directed by George Devine and starring Sir John Gielgud and Dame Peggy Ashcroft, in 1955. Of this production experience Noguchi recalled,

> I was able to do it by this flow of sets which are being moved around all the time without one seeing who is moving them. They were not being moved mechanically, but by people inside or behind them. There was an improvisational quality to the performance. It annoyed the British to no end. It infuriated them. They thought I had betrayed Shakespeare. For a while I was a hero, and people adored me when I went to England, but not after I designed *King Lear*. Of course, they also attacked Kurosawa after his film *Ran* premiered, which was an adaptation of *King Lear*, however in a Japanese context. I was very careful about designing *King Lear* properly. It had a perfectly logical flow. You see, there are actually 26 changes in *King Lear*.

As Lincoln Kirstein noted, however, it was Martha Graham and Isamu Noguchi who had the most satisfactory artistic collaboration in the tradition of Serge Diaghilev in Paris: recruiting twentieth century artists whose focus was not primarily theatrical to design his dance productions.

By 1948, Noguchi had executed designs for twenty dances, fifteen of which were for Graham including, among others, *Frontier, Chronicle, El Penitente, Hérodiade, Appala-*

6

chian Spring, Dark Meadow, Cave of the Heart, Night Journey, Errand into the Maze, and Diversion of Angels. These works, and the Balanchine and Stravinsky production of Orpheus, which all incorporated Noguchi's set designs, were modern choreographic masterworks.

For all intents and purposes, the choreographic career of Martha Graham spanned the entire 20th century. From a historical dance perspective, one can say that Martha Graham created at least one significant dance every year from 1929 to 1943, beginning with her first masterpiece, Heretic (1929), and continuing with Lamentation (1930), Primitive Mysteries (1931), Satiric Festival Song (1932), Ekstasis (1933), Celebration (1934), Frontier (1935), Chronicle (1936)[2], Immediate Tragedy (1937), Deep Song (1937), American Document (1938), Every Soul Is a Circus (1939), Letter to the World (1940), Punch and the Judy (1941), Salem Shore (1943), and Deaths and Entrances (1943).

Graham reached her choreographic pinnacle, with eight first-rate works all danced in sculptural spaces designed by Noguchi, between the years 1944-48: El Penitente (1944)[3], Appalachian Spring (1944), Hérodiade (1944), Dark Meadow (1946), Cave of the Heart (1946), Night Journey (1947), Errand Into the Maze (1947), and Diversion of Angels (1948)[4].

In the Fifties, Noguchi's sculptures were incorporated into Graham's Judith (1950), Voyage (1953), Seraphic Dialogue (1955), Clytemnestra, and Embattled Garden (both

1958). During the Sixties, Graham's choreographic output consisted of minor classic dances such as Alcestis (1960), Acrobats of God (1960), Phaedra (1962), Circe (1963), created for dancer Mary Hinkson, and Cortege of Eagles (1967). Noguchi designed sets which enabled Graham, who was then in her seventies and in physical decline, to appear onstage in all of these works.

Graham reluctantly retired from performing in 1969. From 1973 until 1990, she continued to choreograph new dances, such as Maple Leaf Rag (1990), and re-work old pieces, but only Acts of Light (1981) and Rite of Spring (1984) can compare with the rest of the major works in the Graham repertory. Although the Graham/Noguchi collaboration ended in 1967, in her final years Graham recycled three of Noguchi's set designs, using them in Judith (1980), Phaedra's Dream (1983), and Night Chant (1988), the last dance Noguchi saw before he died.

Isamu Noguchi and Martha Graham's extended collaboration perpetuated in America Diaghilev's belief in using visual artists' designs for dance. Indeed, twenty of the dances designed by Noguchi are still in active repertoire. Two of today's most influential modern choreographers, Merce Cunningham and Paul Taylor, were members of Martha Graham's company, and both were inspired and influenced by Graham's long-running artistic relationship with the sculptor. Each has actively sought to involve visual artists in the designing of his dances. The most obvious collaborations in this lineage are

Cunningham with Robert Rauschenberg and Taylor with Alex Katz.

Rauschenberg, who has designed approximately forty sets for dances by Merce Cunningham, Paul Taylor, and Trisha Brown since the early Fifties, said, "Noguchi did a great job of putting sculpture in dance. He also had a great sense of monumental drama, and that went with Martha Graham's heavy-handed mythological indulgences. That is what I was working away from when I began designing for Merce and Paul. I wanted to open up the space."

From 1955 to 1965, Rauschenberg designed approximately twenty dances for Cunningham. Said Rauschenberg, "I know—I think—one of the reasons Merce started making his own costumes was after an experience with Noguchi, while he was dancing with Graham in *El Penitente*, I believe.* He couldn't breathe because he was wearing a Noguchi mask that he had to hold on to with his teeth. You can see if you were a really great dancer that it would be an obstacle."

Rauschenberg designed *Travelogue* for the Merce Cunningham Dance Company in 1978. "That was about a ten-year break from Merce, wasn't it? It was a joy," Rauschenberg recalled, "because I had matured or developed in a way that made everything a lot fresher, for me at least. What also happened was that Merce's possibilities were grander. I think we both spread because of some kind of prestige or just physical space."

As for his own collaborative efforts in designing for dance, Rauschenberg explained,

I think the most successful collaboration was with Jasper [Johns] and myself collaborating with Paul [Taylor for *The Tower*]. I also work very well with Trisha [Brown]. We share a lot of previous experiences. I think she has a kind of disorganized courage, that energy level and surprise in her choreography. Trisha kept that sense of humor that was so unique from the Judson days. Because Merce and I would collaborate on postcards, neither one of us would go into much detail: A fact would be how long the dance is, how many people are in the dance, and then some of Merce's stick figures. And Merce has always worked that way, with John [Cage], too.[5] Nobody can work with John. He does what he does and that is it. I have a further limitation in that nobody ever trips over the music, but if you put a costume on somebody that has a restriction, no matter how good the idea is, then you have ruined the dance. I try to do things that the body can hang around naked inside. If you are designing for dancers, you have to have a great respect for the human body.

Responding to Noguchi's observation that designing for dance is about space,

* Merce Cunningham had a similar experience when he choreographed *The Seasons* for Balanchine's Ballet Society. See page 103.

Rauschenberg replied, "It's about space and breath."

Other visual artists who design for dance often say that when they begin their projects they have to think about Noguchi, and then Rauschenberg. Alex Katz, who designed fifteen dances for Paul Taylor over a twenty-year period beginning in 1960, has said that it was Taylor who educated him about collaborations. Katz was given complete license and freedom by Taylor who, Katz once stated, "would try anything, so great was his self-assurance, but who would be capable of throwing out an entire set on opening night."

While Katz's collaboration with Taylor has ended, he continues to design for David Parsons, a Taylor company alumnus. About his own odyssey in designing for dance Katz said, "When I focused on dance I had to think about Noguchi and Bob Rauschenberg. They were the two really good stage artists. Most of the artists just go for flats. But they were both 'object' people. I think Paul and me were of the same time period as Martha and Noguchi were."

In the Seventies, Noguchi was commissioned to design the Martha Graham Dance Theater at the University of California at Los Angeles. This was to be an experimental performance theater for the Martha Graham Dance Company as well as an exhibition space for all thirty-five dance sets created by Noguchi. Unfortunately, the project was abandoned, but the model can be seen at the Isamu Noguchi Garden Museum in Long Island City, New York. Reflecting on the project, Noguchi said, "I would

like very much to do it, sure, if there is a possibility of doing it. I thought of it as a kind of memory of Martha—and Bucky [Buckminster Fuller], too. I have Bucky's geodesic dome on top. After all, Martha comes from California.[6] She is very much from Santa Barbara. Also something for me: I come from California, too."

In the meantime, Noguchi worked on other large-scale projects. Between the years 1971 to 1979, he created fountains for the Supreme Court in Tokyo, the Society of Four Arts in Palm Beach, and the Art Institute of Chicago. In addition, "Playscapes," his first U. S. playground, opened in Atlanta, and several public sculptures were installed: "Void," for Pepsico (Purchase, NY), "Shinto," for the Bank of Tokyo (New York City; dismantled 1980-81), and "Landscape of Time" at the Seattle Federal Building. "Tengoku" ("Heaven"), an interior garden and granite pylon for the Sogetsu Flower Arranging School in Tokyo, was completed. A granite sculpture, "The Spirit of the Lima Bean," was erected in Costa Mesa, California, as part of an overall landscape project called "California Scenario," which was completed between 1981-83.

Noguchi was eighty years old when his museum opened in 1984. He invested almost $3 million of his own money in the project. The Isamu Noguchi Garden Museum is dedicated to the exhibition of his sculptural works, some of which he bought back from their owners so that they could form a part of the museum's collection.

"As far as I'm concerned, I didn't particularly

9

want to build a museum," Noguchi said. "It is by no means an ego trip. It was out of necessity that I was driven to do it. Generally I find a disinterest—an antagonism—with most museum curators and collectors because museum ownership is more or less based on value, really the money system, evaluation. That is why art is so popular now because it ties into the way of art as a well-known affair. It has become incorporated. On the one hand, I didn't expect to have any kind of special treatment from them. On the other hand, I think I deserve this museum."

The 24,000-square foot gallery space and rock garden had been used years before by a photoengraving business and was a junkyard when Noguchi acquired the property. About this most personal creation for the public Noguchi said, "I didn't know any museum that wanted to devote the space I would need if I were to have some kind of explanation of what I was trying to do in my work. You see, my work could be passed into a museum's basement for whatever purpose. That is why I am not sympathetic to what museums are trying to do. My museum is not an ordinary museum. It is a partisan museum. I don't know if it was such a good thing to do but I felt obliged to do it, that is all. I'm trying to beat my own drum."

Noguchi remodeled the property in 1983, transforming it into a museum space with the help of architect and friend Soji Sadao. There are fourteen different sections in the gallery. "The areas are all different aspects of the same thing," Noguchi explained. "I don't say that I lay a law down as to how to do things. It is always a discovery. Each time is different. If it isn't different there is no interest. In nature, everything is different. No two things are alike because of the circumstances of the genetics of the interaction with whatever comes along. If things are standardized now because of industrialization, well, we are killing nature. Nature in us is atrophied. We begin to want to see things that way, machine-made, like automobiles. I think that is why we prefer things which have been transformed industrially: To make them not touched by human hands." In the museum brochure Noguchi wrote, "This garden museum is a metaphor for the world and how an artist attempted to influence its becoming." Said Noguchi, "I don't say that I'm at the end of my changes. I do what I do with the hope of bringing it out in the open. You see, it depends on how you are and what your attitude is. There are no hard and fixed rules." When asked about his ability to ensure the museum's future once it was established, Noguchi replied, "I can't. It's a kind of worry. It's a worry in any case. Suppose you do nothing? Eventually then you die. And then they start quarreling over to whom it is going to go. Then the government comes along and sees themselves to some of it. Where does it stay? Suppose it does land in a museum or is auctioned someplace. Who owns it? It's a very dubious future in any case."

Indeed, Noguchi continued to produce a prodigious body of work throughout the Eighties. During this period, the sculpture "To The Issei" and the plaza for the Japanese American Cultural and Community Center in Los Angeles were completed; "Constellation for Louis Kahn," a sculpture, was installed at the Kimball Art Museum in Texas in 1983; the Domon Ken Museum water garden in Japan was completed; a large-scale public sculpture, "Memorial To Benjamin Franklin," originally proposed in 1933, and later re-proposed to the Philadelphia Museum of Art, was installed in 1984; the sculpture garden for the Museum of Fine Arts in Houston was completed and dedicated in 1986; and in 1985, Noguchi was invited to represent the United States at the 1986 Venice Biennale, where he would show, among other things, new *Akari* and a ten-foot high marble slide originally conceived in 1966. Also in 1986, his fountain "Tsukubai" was realized and installed at the Metropolitan Museum of Art in New York City.

What is astonishing is that Noguchi felt that he had always had "forlorn" art periods: the Thirties, the Forties, the Fifties and the Eighties. He said, "I've always been by myself. I've always felt myself as a kind of immigrant, certainly outside."

Yet his collaboration with Martha Graham lasted almost half a century. The phenomenal artistic achievements of Noguchi and Graham were continuously stimulated by a convergence of experience, and the affinities of mind, philosophy, dreams, and erudition kept them in perpetual motion. As Noguchi said, "Art to me is clearly a factor in being alive."

1 Dating from the Kofun period (circa AD 250-552), Haniwa are large, cylindrical, hollow baked red clay sculptures, sometimes in the form of animals, birds and humans, which were placed around the tombs of the imperial family and important members of the royal court.
2 Noguchi designed the sets for *Frontier* and *Chronicle.*
3 Noguchi redesigned the set. The original was by Arch Lauterer.
4 The Noguchi set for *Diversion of Angels* was used in performance only once.
5 John Milton Cage, Jr. (1912-1992). American avant-garde composer.
6 Martha Graham was born in Allegheny, Pennsylvania, on May 11, 1894. The family moved to Santa Barbara in 1909. Graham relocated to New York City in 1921 where she lived until her death on April 1, 1991.

37 PRINCIPAL SET DESIGNS FOR
DANCE AND THEATRE

TITLE	YEAR	CHOREOGRAPHER
At the Hawk's Well	*1926*	*Michio Ito*
The Expanding Universe	*1932*	*Ruth Page*
Frontier	*1935*	*Martha Graham*
Chronicle	*1936*	*Martha Graham*
El Penitente (re-design)	*1944*	*Martha Graham*
Imagined Wing	*1944*	*Martha Graham*
Hérodiade	*1944*	*Martha Graham*
Appalachian Spring	*1944*	*Martha Graham*
John Brown	*1945*	*Erick Hawkins*
Dark Meadow	*1946*	*Martha Graham*
The Bells	*1946*	*Ruth Page*
Cave of the Heart	*1946*	*Martha Graham*
Shut Not Your Doors	*1946*	*Yuriko*
Stephen Acrobat	*1947*	*Erick Hawkins*
Errand into the Maze	*1947*	*Martha Graham*
Night Journey	*1947*	*Martha Graham*
The Seasons	*1947*	*Merce Cunningham*
Tale of Seizure	*1948*	*Yuriko*

TITLE	YEAR	CHOREOGRAPHER
Orpheus	*1948*	*George Balanchine*
Wilderness Stair (Diversion of Angels)	*1948*	*Martha Graham*
Judith	*1950*	*Martha Graham*
Voyage	*1953*	*Martha Graham*
Theater of a Voyage	*1955*	*Martha Graham*
Seraphic Dialogue	*1955*	*Martha Graham*
King Lear	*1955*	*Royal Shakespeare Company*
Clytemnestra	*1958*	*Martha Graham*
Embattled Garden	*1958*	*Martha Graham*
Acrobats of God	*1960*	*Martha Graham*
Alcestis	*1960*	*Martha Graham*
Phaedra	*1962*	*Martha Graham*
Circe	*1963*	*Martha Graham*
Cortege of Eagles	*1967*	*Martha Graham*
Variable Landscape	*1978*	*Kei Takei*
Judith	*1980*	*Martha Graham*
Phaedra's Dream	*1983*	*Martha Graham*
God's Angry Men	*1984*	*Erick Hawkins*
Night Chant	*1988*	*Martha Graham*

ISAMU NOGUCHI
DANCE DESIGNS AND COMMENTARY

Isamu Noguchi's commentary on his dance designs was compiled from dialogues conducted with the sculptor from 1983 to 1988.

The original program notes were researched and compiled at the Library and Museum of the Performing Arts at Lincoln Center in New York City.

Mr. Noguchi's written excerpts were compiled from his monograph A Sculptor's World *(Harper & Row, N.Y., 1968).*

The relationship of dance to its ambiance is important, which is why I do sets. To me, dance is an extension of a sculptural air—the air we happen to sit around in. Merely to say that dance is another form of art is not enough. Art is more than what one happens to be looking at.

— Isamu Noguchi

AT THE HAWK'S WELL

by William Butler Yeats

Noguchi's first designs for dance—papier maché masks—were executed for Michio Ito's 1926 production of *At the Hawk's Well,* the Nōh-influenced play by Yeats. Said Noguchi, "I don't know whether he ever used them or whatever happened to them. At the same time I did a head of him, and that I have at the museum."

NOTES

Through Ito, a Japanese Dalcrozian-trained dancer who had known Yone Noguchi, Isamu Noguchi secured introductions to artists in Paris, notably Foujita.

According to Helen Caldwell in Michio Ito—The Dancer and the Dance *(University of California Press, May 1975), Ito, while in London, entered into an association with William Butler Yeats which was to have a profound influence on Ito's dance. Ito assisted Yeats, along with Ezra Pound, in the production of Yeats's* At the Hawk's Well—*an Irish play in the Japanese Nōh style. It was presented in London in April 1916 with Ito in the role of The Guardian of the Well, for which he created a dance somewhat in the Nōh tradition. He also set the movements for the other actors and the chorus and introduced Yeats and Pound to Utai, the singing element of the Nōh drama. Ito was so impressed by the poetic beauty and dramatic power of* At the Hawk's Well, *he presented it at least twice in the United States, in New York City in 1918 and in California in 1929; and then again in Japan in 1939 because he regarded it as a genuine Nōh play.*

THE EXPANDING UNIVERSE

Choreography by Ruth Page
Music by Robert Wolf
Costume by Isamu Noguchi

Premiered November 2, 1932
Fargo, North Dakota
New York premiere: January 29, 1933
John Golden Theatre, New York
Performed by Ruth Page

"... The first thing I did after finding a studio was to make *Miss Expanding Universe*, so-named by Buckminster Fuller. And with enthusiasm I tried to persuade Theremin[1], who is considered the father of electronic music, to produce "New Music" with his electronic instrument, playing for him the many *Gagaku* records I had brought back. I suggested that Martha Graham should take part and that Theremin rods be placed at different points on the stage to become activated as the dancer moved. Nothing resulted."

NOTES

In her autobiography Page by Page *(New York: Dance Horizons, 1978), Ruth Page wrote, "... I (being in my sack, mask, and stick period) danced* Expanding Universe *in a Noguchi sack...."[2]*

That "sack" was Noguchi's interpretation of his own 1931 sculpture, which Buckminster Fuller called "Miss Expanding Universe," which was inspired by Haniwa figures. Noguchi and Fuller also referred to Ruth Page as "Miss Expanding Universe."

This sack bears a resemblance to the stretch fabric dress worn by Martha Graham in Lamentation *(1930). Since Noguchi's sister, Ailes Gilmour, was a member of the Martha Graham Group from 1930-33, it is probable that he saw Graham perform this solo.*

FROM THE ORIGINAL PROGRAM NOTES

"To those who are plastically minded this dance, which is done entirely inside of a jersey sack, will seem to be a series of startling poses. To the philosophically minded, the dance will seem the continuous struggle of mankind through calmness and strife to expand into new ideas and new forms ending in the complete mystery which is the universe."

FRONTIER[3]

Choreography by Martha Graham
Music by Louis Horst
Set by Isamu Noguchi
Costume by Martha Graham

Premiered April 28, 1935
Guild Theatre, New York
Performed by Martha Graham

"To me, objects are quite incidental and used only as a convenience. A prop is a prop. I'm talking about something beyond that—something that permeates space.

"In 1935 I did *Frontier*. I used a rope, nothing else. It's not the rope that is the sculpture, but it is the space which it creates that is the sculpture. I used the space of the stage and the whole space above it, which was an innovation. It is an illusion of space. It is not flat like a painting used as a backdrop—it is a three-dimensional perspective. It bisects the theater space, therefore it creates the whole box into a spatial concept. And it is in that spatial concept that Martha moves and creates her dances. In that sense, Martha is a sculptor herself.

"I think of Martha's total dance as a development in a certain direction. Starting in one way, and then shifting ground, perhaps, but still in a direction that one can call 'sculptural.' In that sense, Martha's ballet *Primitive Mysteries* (1931) is a bisection of space, very vigorously hewed. A cut, rather than molded. That is sculpture. I'm glad to hear it called sculptural. . . .

"I believe we had to find a dance theater with an emotionally-charged space which, of course, is sculpture. It is the sculpture of space and it is not about objects. Martha moved in that sculptural space. It is correct to say that she was concerned with space rather than with painting. Painting, as a backdrop, is an assimilation of reality which sculpture overrides. Sculpture is reality itself. I conceive of sculpture as a permeation of space. I believe that's how Martha treated it."

NOTES:

Noguchi wrote, "Frontier was my first set. It was for me the genesis of an idea—to wed the total void of theater space to form and action. A rope, running from the two top corners of the proscenium to the floor rear center of the stage, bisected the three-dimensional void of stage space. This seemed to throw the entire volume of air straight over the heads of the audience.

"At the rear convergence was a small section of log fence, to start from and to return to. The white ropes created a curious ennobling—of an outburst into space and, at the same time, of the public's inrush toward infinity.

"This set was the point of departure for all my subsequent theater work: space became a volume to be dealt with sculpturally."

FROM THE ORIGINAL PROGRAM NOTES:

Graham called Frontier "an American perspective of the Plains." Later she added, "The pioneer woman still typifies to us the vision and courage of those who extended our frontiers and established our heritage."

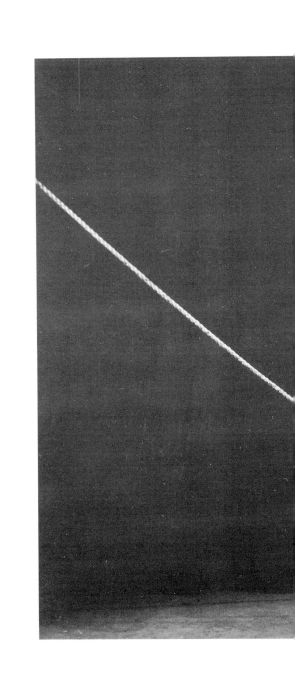

CHRONICLE

Choreography by Martha Graham
Music by Wallingford Riegger
Set by Isamu Noguchi
Costumes by Martha Graham

Premiered December 20, 1936
The Guild Theatre, New York
Performed by Martha Graham and Group

"*Chronicle* consisted of a manipulation of the stage space with drops. I used spatial division through flats and light, a kind of curtain. Martha was not dependent on sets. These were dances without sets. In fact, most dances had no sets. My doing *Frontier* (1935) was an innovation for the modern dance. Modern dancers just danced on the stage at YMHA or someplace. The only props they ever had was a stool or something to stand on, something like that. That is all. As I said, using the space of the stage, the whole space above it, was an innovation. *Chronicle*, I wasn't probably ready for, and I don't think it was ever done with my set after that. *Chronicle* was performed just once."

FROM THE ORIGINAL PROGRAM NOTES

"Chronicle *does not attempt to show the actualities of war; rather does it, by evoking war's images, set forth the fateful prelude to war, portray the devastation of spirit which it leaves in its wake, and suggest an answer.*"

The dance included the sections "Dances Before Catastrophe," "Dances After Catastrophe," and "Prelude to Action."

EL PENITENTE

Choreography by Martha Graham
Music by Louis Horst
Original set design by Arch Lauterer, redesigned by Noguchi (1944)
Costumes by Edythe Gilfond

Premiered August 11, 1940
Bennington College Theatre, Bennington, Vermont
Redesigned production performed May 7-14, 1944
National Theatre, New York
Performed by Martha Graham, Erick Hawkins and Merce Cunningham

"I redesigned *El Penitente* because Martha wasn't especially happy with the first designs. The Flagellants was the theme of *El Penitente*. Martha's and Erick's interpretation came from the Christian element in the rites of Penitente, which is something like Ayatollah Khomeini and his group in Iran."

NOTES
Yuriko, a member of the Martha Graham Company (1944-67), helped sew the sail Noguchi designed for the 1944 production. In her opinion, El Penitente *became a completely new production because of the sail, the cross, the cart, and the mask that Noguchi created for the dance.*

FROM THE ORIGINAL PROGRAM NOTES
"The Penitentes of the Southwest are a sect which believes in the purification from sin through severe penance. Even today, in both Old and New Mexico, they practice their ancient rites, including the Crucifixion. The dance bears no factual relationship to these practices but is presented as a story told after the manner of old mystery (minstrel) plays. The three figures enter, assume their characters and perform as a group of players. The action is divided by a return to the entrance theme. The Festival Dance at the end is a version of a popular dance of celebration without ritualistic content as in the preceding scenes."

© Louis Peres

© Nan Melville

IMAGINED WING

Choreography by Martha Graham
Music by Darius Milhaud, "Jeux du Printemps"
Set by Isamu Noguchi
Costumes by Edythe Gilfond

Premiered October 30, 1944
Library of Congress, Washington, D.C.
Performed by the Martha Graham Company
in honor of the eightieth birthday of Elizabeth Sprague Coolidge

"*Imagined Wing* just didn't gel together with the Milhaud music like *Appalachian Spring* and *Hérodiade* did [with their scores]. *Imagined Wing* was the least interesting of the three. I would say *Chronicle, Imagined Wing,* and later *Diversion of Angels* didn't quite make it. They were a 'searching.' I was always a bit experimental, and if one does experimental work, one can't expect to hit it all the time. There have to be mistakes.

"As for my using mistakes, well, I know better than to repeat it, for one thing. In the case of *Imagined Wing,* there was a symmetrical object which detracted from the dancers. It was locked into a spot and there was no way of escaping from it. Western art tends toward the symmetrical, Eastern art toward the asymmetrical. Just look at flower arranging in Japan: It is about asymmetry, not symmetry.

"I remember seeing Diaghilev's Ballet Russes in Paris. There was one piece with a motion picture projection and it had a disquieting effect on me. The use of stage space as an asymmetrical expanse where the dancer moves—thus the viewer moves—has infinite possibilities. The asymmetrical play of emotions on the stage is understood by the audience as space definition, even if they don't move around themselves. Because Martha was moving around, the audience is able to imagine themselves by moving their awareness from one spot to the next. Even though they are seated there, their imagination is not stuck there. I think generally I exploited that pretty well."

NOTES

The cast members were Merce Cunningham, Nina Fonaroff, Erick Hawkins, Pearl Lang, Marjorie Mazia, May O'Donnell and Yuriko; Martha Graham was not in the dance. Yuriko, who portrayed The Page and

Wall and seat from Herodiade *(similar to the wall in* Imagined Wing, *according to Yuriko, who performed in the dance)*

changed the scenery during the dance, said, "For Imagined Wing Noguchi designed a wall like there was in Hérodiade. But in Imagined Wing the wall could fan out like a folded origami screen that separates a room or an area, and the dancers would come from behind it. It was a different way for Noguchi to expand the space. Perhaps this central piece was too stationary, according to what Mr. Noguchi said."

FROM THE ORIGINAL PROGRAM NOTES
"Graham deemed Imagined Wing 'A fantasy of theatre with several characters in various imagined places.'"

HÉRODIADE

(Originally titled Mirror Before Me, *from Stéphane Mallarmé)*
Choreography by Martha Graham
Music by Paul Hindemith, "Hérodiade de Stéphane Mallarmé, récitation orchestrale"
Set by Isamu Noguchi
Costumes Edythe Gilfond

Premiered October 30, 1944
Library of Congress, Washington, D.C.
Performed by Martha Graham and May O'Donnell

"I never subscribed to the idea that sculptures are just sculptures and not something that is a tool. These are symbolic or gestural tools Martha was using. They were an extension of her body. It's my own approach to sculpture—as being part of living, not just part of art. I don't look at art as something separate and sacrosanct. It's part of usefulness. My relationship with Martha is purely that of sculpture. It's probably why I was able to do those things. Also, if you look at what I was doing outside the theater at that particular time, it often relates to what I did in the theater. Again, it was a very similar kind of thing I was doing in sculpture. Back and forth, back and forth. It is difficult to say *Hérodiade* is Greek. It is Biblical. Especially with *Hérodiade*, I used an interest that I already had elsewhere—the skeleton of the body."

NOTES

Noguchi called this dance "the most baroque and specifically sculptural of my sets. Within a woman's private world, and intimate space, I was asked to place a mirror, a chair, and a clothes rack. Salome dances before her mirror. What does she see? Her bones, the potential skeleton of her body. The chair is like an extension of her vertebrae; the clothes rack, the circumscribed bones on which is hung her skin. This is the desecration of beauty, the consciousness of time."

FROM THE ORIGINAL PROGRAM NOTES

"The scene is an antechamber where a woman waits with her attendant. She does not know for what she waits; she does not know what she may be required to do or endure, and the time of waiting becomes a time of preparation. A mirror provokes an anguish of scrutiny; images of the past, fragments of dreams float to its cold surface, add to the woman's agony of consciousness. With self-knowledge comes accep-

tance of her mysterious destiny: this is the moment when waiting ends.

Solemnly, the attendant prepares her. As she advances to meet the unknown, the curtain falls."

"The piece on stage left is a human body in a certain aspect. The chair is the chair of memories that Plato speaks about. When you sit in the chair of memories, if you're strong enough and you've drunk deep enough of the river of memories in the underworld, you will remember not only the actual fact, but you will remember the past of thousands of years ago. And that mirror that stands on stage right, when I looked in that mirror I saw my finish. I saw my beginning and I saw my finish."—Martha Graham

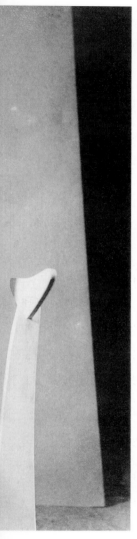

APPALACHIAN SPRING

Choreography by Martha Graham
Music by Aaron Copland
Set by Isamu Noguchi
Costumes by Edythe Gilfond

Premiered October 30, 1944
Library of Congress, Washington, D.C.
Performed by Martha Graham and Company

"*Appalachian Spring* wasn't a symmetrical setting at all. It was based on diagonals that come from the rear and stage right. The seat, or 'the woman's place,' in *Appalachian Spring* is actually a Shaker rocking chair, a seat which is also a sculpture or a sculpture which may be sat on. The experience of sculpture is not only by sight. The tactile quality of sculpture is surely as important as the visual to cause thought.

"*Appalachian Spring* was Martha's movement toward Americana. This work had to do with the land and the settlers. The idea was about building a new land, new life, and new hope. As a matter of fact, I saw a movie on a plane about a little boy in a Shaker community building a church, putting the rafters up, and this, and that, and the other. It composed a very nice movie, actually, the idea of building. Now, of course, we are overwhelmed by developers. There is a mania that is taking hold.

"I think it was wonderful that both Nureyev and Baryshnikov danced the two lead roles in that dance ["The Preacher" and "The Husbandman," respectively] which were created by Merce Cunningham and Erick Hawkins. It was a brilliant homage to Martha and tied the whole dance into one thing. It is not modern, it is not ballet—it is Dance. It is timeless."

NOTES

Noguchi wrote of this dance, "New land, new home, new life; a testament to the American settler, a folk theater. I attempted through the elimination of all non-essentials to arrive at an essence of the stark pioneer spirit, that essence which flows out to permeate the stage. It is empty but full at the same time. It is like Shaker furniture."

FROM THE ORIGINAL PROGRAM NOTES

"*The range of the Appalachian Mountains provided one of the first frontiers in American history. The*

© Arnold Eagle

© Nan Melville

early pioneers went into this beautiful and abundant wilderness to settle, to build houses and cultivate the newly-cleared land, and to raise their families in remote and lonely isolation, their only visitor an occasional wandering preacher. These preachers, often fanatic in temper, preached a doctrine of austerity, condemned all earthly pleasures as evil, described the imagined horrors of hell and damnation and left, at the end of their sermons, very little comfort in everyday life.

"Appalachian Spring *is a folk tale set in the Appalachian wilderness at this period of American history. Its characters are a young pioneer and his bride, a pioneer woman, a wandering preacher and his small band of ecstatic followers. The ballet tells, in lyric terms, of the young couple's wedding day, the building of their house, their celebration, the preacher's dire sermon and the pioneer woman's gentle blessing, and the day ends as they start their life together."*

FROM ANOTHER VERSION

"Part and parcel of our lives is that moment of Pennsylvania spring when there was 'a garden eastward in Eden.'

"Spring was celebrated by a man and a woman building a house with joy and love and prayer; by a revivalist and his followers in their shouts of exaltation; by a pioneering woman with her dreams of the Promised Land."

JOHN BROWN

Choreography by Erick Hawkins
Music by Charles Mills
Libretto by Erick Hawkins
Poetic text by Robert Richman
Set by Isamu Noguchi
Costume by Erick Hawkins

Premiered May 16, 1945
National Theatre, New York
Performed by Erick Hawkins as "The Abolitionist, Captain John Brown" and the Martha Graham Company
with Stuart Hodes as the "Interlocutor"

Revived in 1984 as God's Angry Men, *a passion play of John Brown. See page 200.*

"I remember very well designing *John Brown,* which was Hawkins's homage to the anti-slavery crusade. Erick came to me with these notions and I was glad to help him. He always held it against me that we just didn't continue. Well, I'm my own jag, and it is only when I'm led by a continuous line of development, like with Martha, which makes it interesting for me."

NOTES
   Upon his death in 1994, Mr. Hawkins bequeathed this set to the Noguchi Museum, where it is exhibited.

FROM THE ORIGINAL PROGRAM NOTES
   A quote from Thoreau was included in the first program description: "I am here to plead his cause with you. I plead not for his life, but for his character—his immortal life; and so it becomes your cause wholly, and it is not his in the least."

FROM A LATER PROGRAM
   "A few months after the hanging of John Brown, James Redpath published a biography of him with this dedication:
   'To Wendell Phillips, Emerson and Thoreau,
   Who, when the mob cried, "Madman!"

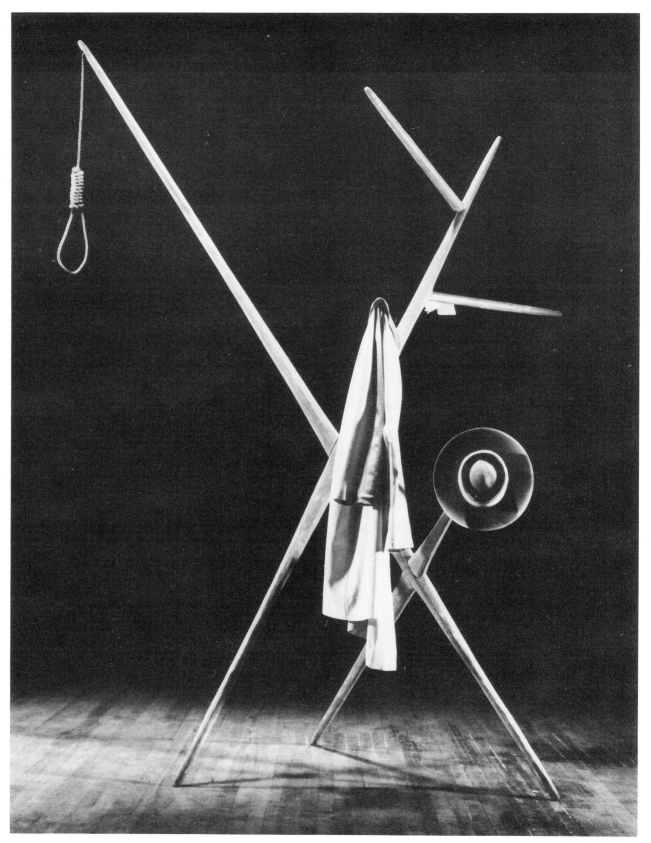

said, "Saint!"'

"In the dance, the Interlocutor reflects the many contemporary reactions to John Brown's beliefs and principles, such as those of Thoreau or of Frederick Douglass—the Negro Abolitionist leader once a slave— or of Senator Mason of Virginia, or of Colonel Preston in charge of his execution. The Interlocutor also speaks as a modern Chorus, who with its further view evaluates and interprets John Brown.

"In the Civil War, which freed four million slaves, one million men on the two sides were killed. Whether any goal of freedom has to be reached through such destruction has always been a challenging enigma in the world's history.

"The core of this passion play is the rise to spiritual greatness of Brown, who, defeated in his faulty attempt to defeat slavery by force of arms, came to recognize the power of the spirit within, and walked as one blindfolded, in devotion only to principle, even to the gallows."

DARK MEADOW

Choreography by Martha Graham
Music by Carlos Chávez, "Hija de Colquide" (1944)
Set by Isamu Noguchi
Costumes by Edythe Gilfond

Premiered January 23, 1946
Plymouth Theatre, New York
Performed by Martha Graham and Company

"*Dark Meadow* is a very important work about the external adventures of seeking and is definitely part of Martha's so-called 'Greek cycle.' *Dark Meadow* has to do with the primordial time of the mind. These are spaces of the mind that Martha is dealing with. These are situations of birth and renewal—mysteries, you might say.

"*Dark Meadow* is a primal piece for me. I didn't need a libretto. It didn't need to have one. When Martha tips the rock over, she puts various symbols that are somewhat Egyptian into the rock. There is a gesture of decision-making. Out of nowhere, out of nothing, something emerges. One thing leads into another and it becomes a flowering. It blossoms.

"The music for *Dark Meadow* was by Chávez. "The Sarabande" in *Dark Meadow* is one of the most beautiful situations of dance that I know of.

"In 1936, I was in Mexico. My first large work was a wall in Mexico, so I was greatly attached to that country, as was Martha. *Dark Meadow* is not specifically Mexican, though. It's more primitive and in the realm of myth. I had the general gist of what *Dark Meadow* was going to be like. After all, we are all more or less aware of each other's interest at the time, and then we are able to transcend our specific time into a general time which is each person's effort. *Dark Meadow* is the key to things that went beyond specific legend to a general, amorphous state of somnolence from which things come. There is a continuity from *Dark Meadow* to *Cave of the Heart* (1946). They are both in an area that I call 'the reality of the mind.'"

NOTES

Noguchi called his set "my homage to Mexico. I made four primordial shapes to define space and as counterpoint to action. They are not stones, but serve the same purpose of suggesting the continuity of time. They move and the world moves." Using the words of Martha Graham he continued, "It is the world

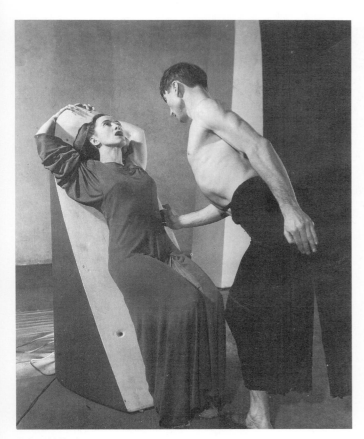

of great symbols, the place of experience, the dark meadow of Ate, the Meadow of choice—the passage to another area of life."

FROM THE ORIGINAL PROGRAM NOTES

"Dark Meadow *is a re-enactment of the Mysteries which attend the eternal adventure of seeking. This dance is the reenactment of the mysteries which attend that adventure:*

Remembrance of the Ancestral Footsteps,—

Terror of Loss,—

Ceaselessness of Love,—

Recurring ecstasy of the Flowering Branch"

FROM THE 1968 REVIVAL PROGRAM NOTES

"Dark Meadow *was first performed on January 23, 1946 at the Plymouth Theatre in New York City. Most of the critics were baffled, if not annoyed, by it. But in* The New Republic, *Stark Young wrote: 'Whether you like* Dark Meadow *or not, and whether you like abstract theatre or not, you have here a chance to see genuine abstract theatre. It is not an imitation of the German theatre of two decades ago, not a vulgar effort toward novelty or shock, but genuine throughout…In Miss Graham's compositions there is often great drawing (as the term is best understood in regard to the art of painting), there is a concentration within the mass density and outline that in itself suggest a certain, as it were, Giottoesque modern. In this regard her composition presents the most creative, strict and nobly designed manifestation of our theatre.'"*

THE BELLS

Choreography by Ruth Page
Music by Darius Milhaud
Libretto by Edgar Allen Poe
Set by Isamu Noguchi
Original costume design by Isamu Noguchi, redesigned in 1950 by Nicholas Remisoff

Premiere April 26, 1946
Chicago Lyric Theatre, Chicago, Illinois
New York premiere September 6, 1946
Performed by the Ballet Russe de Monte Carlo

"I created this church steeple which was built like a marionette. It could collapse. At the end of the performance, the whole thing tumbles down like a wreck. The wires inside, when taut, pull the whole thing together and allow the church steeple to stretch into position. The cathedral I designed for Joan of Arc in Martha's *Seraphic Dialogue* of 1955 came about with the same idea of stretching into position. I think if I hadn't done one, I wouldn't have thought of the other. It is the same principle."

NOTES

Noguchi wrote, "The Bells depicts, within a rhythm of tingling resonance captured from the poem of Edgar Allen Poe, the various aspects of life and decay. The church steeple was a very large prop. Situated stage center rear, it gradually rose and at the end collapsed in a tangled wreck. This was accomplished by articulating it like a puppet. My favorite costumes were those of black bells which, hanging from over their heads, covered everything but the dancers' feet."

Ruth Page wrote, "Practically every newspaper in New York spoke of Noguchi's beautiful skeleton of a church, which he made for The Bells, *and Noguchi's stunning sets for Martha Graham are greatly appreciated in New York. But not one Paris newspaper mentioned Noguchi, who is, I think, our greatest designer for the dance."[4]*

FROM THE ORIGINAL PROGRAM NOTES

"The action of The Bells, *a ballet in five episodes, parallels the psychological development of Edgar Allen Poe's poem, 'The Bells.'*

63

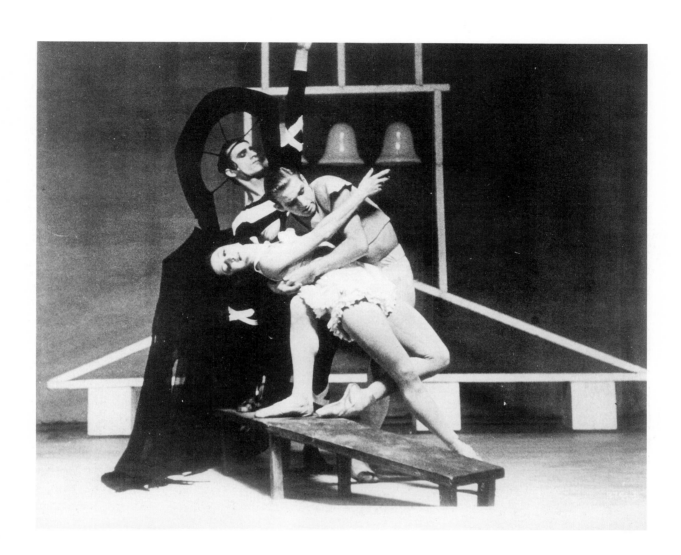

"At the outset all is life, love, and gaiety, but this mood is not allowed to endure. Disintegration and decay set in, until at the end there remains only that peculiar beauty, divorced from truth and moral sense, which is found, according to Poe, in the 'pleasurable sadness' of the contemplation of death and destruction.

"The ballet thus presents a cycle of life, from happiness to obliteration, from illusion to disillusion. The action begins with the entrance of a girl, dressed in bright ornaments, who performs a dance of youthful nonsense to the tinkle of the little Silver Bells. Putting on a wedding veil she dances a happy duet with her Bridegroom, accompanied by the mellow wedding bells, the Golden Bells. Soon the Brazen Bells sound an alarm which disturbs the happiness of the couple. In a solemn interlude the Iron Bells proclaim a discordant, threatening message of futility and impending doom.

"The King of the Ghouls appears to dance a duet with the Bridegroom in which the young man, lured away from his Bride, becomes a victim of the decadence and depravity of a world going mad. As the Bride sees her beloved taken away from her, she covers herself with a dark veil of sorrow, as if to shut out the violence and chaos which surround her. The curtain falls upon the complete triumph of the King of the Ghouls, whose destructive power is epitomized by the collapse into ruin of the church, the symbol of Truth and of Morality. Only the sad beauty of death and disintegration remains."

CAVE OF THE HEART

(Originally titled Serpent Heart*)*
Choreography by Martha Graham
Music by Samuel Barber
Set by Isamu Noguchi
Costumes by Edythe Gilfond

Premiered May 10, 1946 (as Serpent Heart*)*
McMillin Theatre, Columbia University, New York;
Premiered February 27, 1947 as Cave of the Heart
Ziegfeld Theatre, New York
Performed by Martha Graham and Company

"Of course, the legend of Medea is more clearly defined in Martha's *Cave of the Heart,* but it's still an emerging cycle in which Martha wishes to portray an emotional state. Medea was left over from the female goddess period, where snakes prevailed. We started with the snake. The snake is water. It is the passage from which the gods evolve. One finds it, according to my friend Bucky Fuller, in all water-born cultures. It prevailed everywhere, all over the world. The water spiral is a perfect example.

"Martha didn't ask me to make a snake pad from which Medea would emerge. These are objects that I make that derive from a depiction of an emotional state. My sense of sculpture and what art is, is always present. There might be some recollections I might have had from my very frequent visits to museums, whether it's Egyptian or Greek. One finds the worship of the snake from the American Indian all the way to the Greeks. So I used the snake.

"In *Cave of the Heart* Medea dances with a red cloth in her mouth—she is dancing with the snake in her mouth. Then she spews it out of her mouth like blood. You might say, 'Where did she get that?' Well, it's blood. Blood is blood. You'll find with Martha there is quite a continuity as symbols accumulate, which by the time of *Clytemnestra* (1958) are quite recognizable.

"Martha called [her costume] 'the spider dress.' I thought of it as the sun, because Medea was the daughter of the sun. She returned to her origins—Medea is taken away by dragons. Well, the dragons . . . I'm a Dragon, I should know all about it. It has to do with fire and water. The Dragon is the storm—it is the rain, it is the elements. It goes back to the river, to birth.

"Martha was always inventing, using whatever object I gave her. You can call it a prop or a useable thing. The volcanic pad that Medea mounts at the end of the dance, wearing her flaming nimbus dress, is where she disappears. She disappears behind it and when the light comes up, it looks as if she's sinking beyond the horizon like a sunset. The volcanic pad is the volcano, the house, birth. It's the way you go back to life. The five stones leading to the volcano are islands in Greece. They represent the place of passage.

"[Now] they don't use my original designs. They lost them. I think it is terrible what happens to things. One part was thrown into the garbage can. It went into the back of the theater and a truck driver just threw it away."

NOTES

Noguchi wrote, Cave of the Heart is *"a dance of transformation (as in the Nōh drama)." Medea, priestess of the mother goddess, slays the offspring of her union with Jason and is transformed and finally consumed by the flaming nimbus of the setting sun (her father). I constructed a landscape like the islands of Greece. On the horizon (center rear) lies a volcanic shape like a black aorta of the heart; to this lead stepping stone islands. (Jason's voyage, the entry bridge of drama). Opposite (stage left) is coiled a green serpent, on whose back rests the transformation dress of gold (metal)."*

FROM THE ORIGINAL PROGRAM NOTES

"In Greek mythology, Medea was the Princess of Colchis and renowned as a sorceress. She fled from her home with the hero, Jason, to Corinth and lived with him there and bore his children. But Jason was ambitious and when he was offered the hand of the Princess Corinth in marriage he abandoned Medea. Maddened by jealousy, Medea sent the Princess as a wedding gift a poisoned crown which killed her when she put it on. Then Medea destroyed her own children and left Corinth in a chariot drawn by dragons.

"Cave of the Heart is Martha Graham's dramatization of this myth. The action is focussed directly upon the central theme of the myth: the terrible destructiveness of jealousy and of alliance with the dark powers of humanity as symbolized by magic."

FROM ANOTHER VERSION

"This is a dance of possessive and destroying love, a love which feeds upon itself like the serpent heart and, when it is overthrown, is fulfilled only in revenge.

"It is a chronicle much like the myth of Jason, the warrior hero, and Medea, granddaughter of the Sun.

"The One like Medea destroys that which she has been unable to possess and brings upon herself and her beloved the inhuman wrath of one who has been betrayed."

© Philippe Halsman

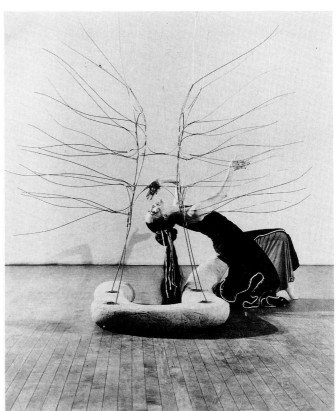

FROM ANOTHER VERSION

"In Greek legend, Medea, was a Princess of Colchis, renowned as a sorceress. She fled from her home with the hero Jason to Corinth where she lived with him as wife and bore him two children. But Jason was ambitious, and when Creon, the King, offered him the hand of his daughter in marriage, he abandoned Medea. Maddened with jealousy, Medea sent the Princess a wedding gift: an enchanted crown. When the Princess placed the crown upon her head, it brought down upon her a terrifying death. Medea then murdered her own children and fled Corinth in a chariot drawn by dragons, returning to her father, the Sun."

SHUT NOT YOUR DOORS

(Title from the poem by Walt Whitman)
Choreography by Yuriko
Music by Roy Harris
Set by Isamu Noguchi
Costume by Yuriko

Premiered October 26, 1946
Needle Trade High School, New York, New York
(Students' Dance Recital, featuring choreography and dancing by Merce Cunningham, Jean Erdman and Yuriko)
Performed by Yuriko

In the summer of 1941 Noguchi drove to California; at the time of the Japanese attack on Pearl Harbor, he was living in Hollywood. In January 1942, aware of anti-Japanese sentiment reaching fevered pitch in California, Noguchi had organized the "Nisei Writers and Artists Mobilized for Democracy," a group which sought to demonstrate the patriotism of Japanese Americans. On February 19, 1942, President Franklin D. Roosevelt signed Executive Order 9066, empowering the Army to round up Japanese Americans living on the Pacific Coast and "evacuate" them to internment camps in remote areas of the West. Of the 110,000 Japanese Americans sent to camps, two-thirds were American citizens. The number would grow to 120,000 internees. Noguchi was persuaded to voluntarily enter the internment camp in Poston, Arizona. "I was immigrant," Noguchi said, "so in the internment camp I not only belonged to an outside group, but I was an outsider of the outside group. Therefore I was doubly removed." He entered the camp in May, only to leave in disgust in November while out on a temporary pass. Noguchi returned to New York, where he established his studio at 33 MacDougal Alley. He had spent seven months as an internee continuously reiterating, "We are all on leave, so to speak."

NOTES

Noguchi designed and built this set for Yuriko, a Japanese American dancer born in San José, California, who was sent to an Arizona internment camp in 1942. A year later she secured government clearance to leave the camp and go to New York, where she began her studies with Martha Graham.

"This dance concerns the emotional struggles of a bewildered woman—one among millions unjustly uprooted —to regain her place in society. Her inner search is difficult, for she experiences the futility of maintaining crushed beliefs until her rediscovery of human freedom and dignity is finally achieved.

Turn O Libertad, for the war is over . . .

Turn your undying face,

To where the future, greater than all the past,

Is swiftly, surely preparing for you.

— Walt Whitman"[5]

In 1996 Yuriko said, "This dance was about the emotional impact of the evacuation. They put Japanese Americans in relocation camps. The ropes represent the fact that we were fenced in by barbed wire. 'Don't shut my door' is how I felt, and I named the dance as such."

STEPHEN ACROBAT

Choreography by Erick Hawkins
Music by Robert Evett
Text by Robert Richman
Set by Isamu Noguchi
Costume by Ken Barr

Premiered February 26, 1947
Ziegfeld Theatre, New York
Performed by the Martha Graham Company, featuring Erick Hawkins and Stuart Hodes

"Actually, the piece I got really involved in with Erick was *Stephen Acrobat,* which came from a metaphysical poem. I used a brightly colored structure for this energetic dance. The tree of knowledge—the apple element has been lost—is one of the two extant elements from *Stephen Acrobat.* The other is the jungle gym."

FROM THE NOGUCHI MUSEUM'S DESCRIPTION OF THE EXHIBITED ELEMENTS OF THE SET
"The narrative of this dance has been described as a parable of the Garden of Eden. An innocent heart is suddenly confronted with the temptation of knowledge, the conscious effort to define good and evil is crushed by the misery and confusion brought about by the loss of its original faith and absolute simplicity."

FROM THE ORIGINAL PROGRAM NOTES
"The theme of the dance is the myth of the Fall. Acrobat is named Stephen—the crowned one: Stephen—the creature who stones himself. Like every acrobat, he has a trainer who has the same name as his own.

I. Paradise
T. Swinging in the golden innocence
Will never end, unless you bend
To hear the yellow song of that tree
Blinding with its fatal fruit.

"Trainer knows that the guilt which Acrobat will suffer from eating of the tree will destroy the freedom and fearlessness of Acrobat's performing life.

II. The Fall

T. "The fear of falling begins to win:

Fear now golden as the air

you swing in.

As one eats ether and begins to swim

Down into the grey whorl, you call,

Call for help but ever fall.

"The fear of being guilty and falling is the narcotic that makes Acrobat actually fall.

III. Hell

A. Where golden air did you turn this black?

T. O Stephen you fool,

You ate from the logical tree.

"Fantasies of sin burden Acrobat with guilt as heavily as actual sin. Stephen's hell is the war his guilt has declared against him.

IV. Paradise

A. O mockery of eating that crippled my eyes!

T. To your Garden of Awakening,

Come swing from black to again white air,

My Stephen Acrobat.

"For all his agony, Acrobat's will to live lets him hear Trainer call him back to that Paradise where there is no good nor evil, and where Acrobat is at one with himself and his trainer."

ERRAND INTO THE MAZE

(Title from a poem by Ben Belitt)
Choreography by Martha Graham
Music by Gian-Carlo Menotti
Set by Isamu Noguchi
Costumes by Martha Graham

Premiered February 28, 1947
Ziegfeld Theatre, New York
Performed by Martha Graham and Mark Ryder

"The minotaur is the image of fear we all must conquer. I designed the minotaur on Erick's head. It was a bull head out of horse hair, like a horse's mane. The depiction is very well done.

"Martha's contribution to *Errand Into the Maze* was the rope, or chord, which is actually a piece of whale gut. She danced around the rope and then tied herself around the pelvic-like structure with it. The chord is part of her dance into the maze. The rope is the thread of Ariadne, which she can manipulate. It is the way out of the maze after you get into it. I used the space division there not as tension, but as objects floating out in space, as a spatial sculpture. It's an idea that can fly off there. It's an idea you happen to see. It's a visible idea. That is what bisects the space. Then there is another rope that is opened a bit. It is not straight. It is vital. It has been pushed aside, like a curtain partially opened so you can see through.

"The two asparagus-like shapes bound together becomes a pelvis. But Martha could take it apart. In Martha's tale, 'Ariadne' is 'Theseus' and out of the maze of the mind is where one finally frees oneself."

NOTES

Noguchi wrote, "The theme, based on the story of the Minotaur, is the extremity we must all face: ourselves. I tried to depict the way, or the labyrinth, as the interior spaces of the mind by means of a rope, as I had done in Frontier. *But this time the effect was altogether different: a space confined like the cave of the mind."*

"The doorway is like supplicant hands, like pelvic bones, from which the child I never had comes forth, but the only child that comes forth is myself"—Martha Graham.

FROM THE ORIGINAL PROGRAM NOTES

"A Greek legend tells of a beast, half-bull, half-man, called the Minotaur, which was kept by the king of Crete in a labyrinth. Every nine years, as a penalty of war, the people of Corinth were doomed to send to Crete fourteen of the city's finest youths and maidens to be fed to the Minotaur.

"The hero, Theseus, prince of Corinth, went himself to Crete and into the labyrinth, guided by a secret thread which had been given to him by the Princess Ariadne, and there fought and killed the Minotaur.

"Martha Graham's Errand Into the Maze derives from this legend. But here the story has been transformed into a drama about the conquest of fear itself. The heroine enters a landscape like the maze of her own heart, goes along the frail thread of her courage to find the fear which lurks like a monster, a Minoatur, within her. She encounters it, conquers it and emerges to freedom."

FROM ANOTHER VERSION

"There is an errand into the maze of the heart's darkness in order to face and do battle with the Creature of Fear. There is the accomplishment of the errand, the instant of triumph, and the emergence from the dark."

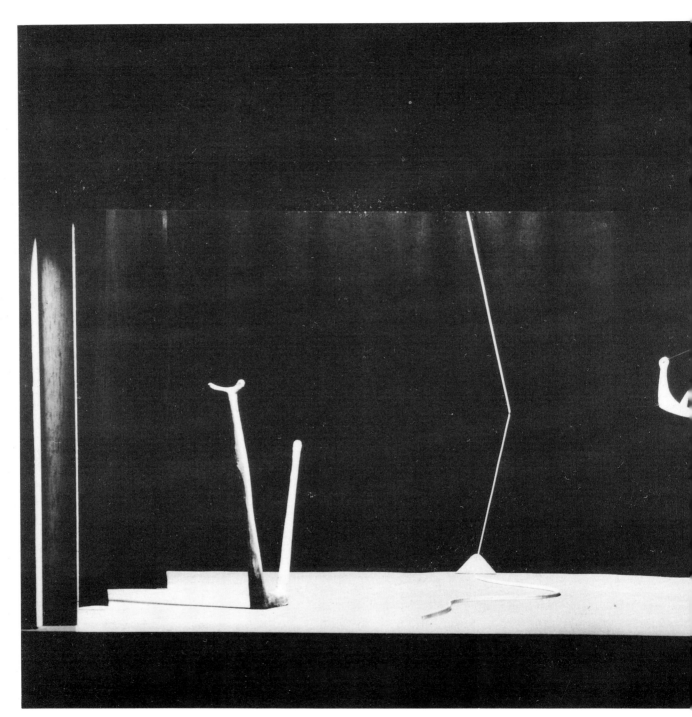

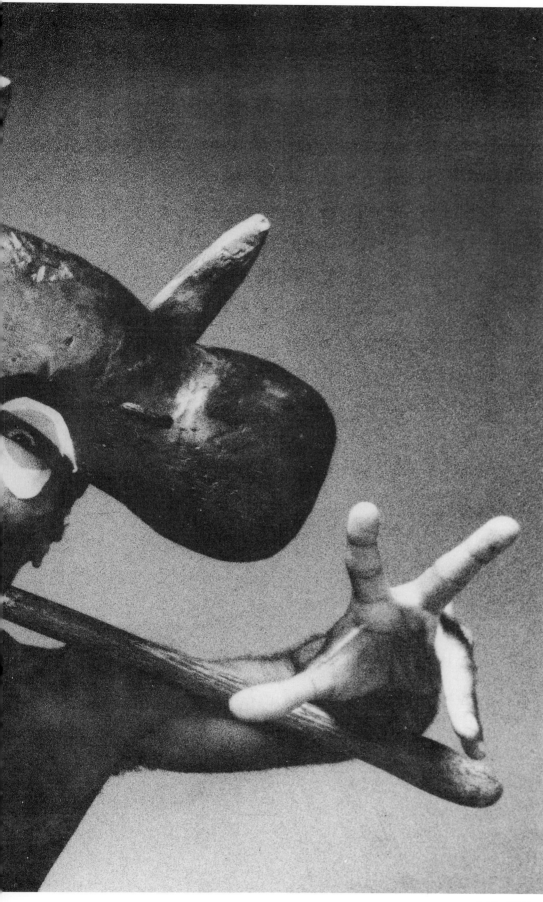

NIGHT JOURNEY

Choreography by Martha Graham
Music by William Schuman
Set by Isamu Noguchi
Costumes by Martha Graham

Premiered May 3, 1947
Cambridge High and Latin School, Cambridge, Massachusetts
Performed by Martha Graham and Company

"The man and woman, or Oedipus and Jocasta, are there in my 'bed,' but in the most rudimentary sense. It is a morphological sculpture. These are not human beings. They are effigies. Human beings are much more dubious and fluid. Of course, we are nothing but a bag of water, but fluid and unpredictable. These are effigies like Cretan goddesses or elemental figures. Martha often says, 'I need a place to sit—a "woman's place" or a bed.' She often needs a place of retreat. You often find in these sets a repetition of somewhat similar uses, from places where they go from to where they go back to. I suppose my contribution is a spatial division. The theater space is not just one level, but it extends way out into the firmament. It is the sculpting of space—the space of the universe where we happen to be.

"There's no question . . . that my beds made Martha get into the most uncomfortable positions. The bed in *Night Journey* is actually two people lying there which is a symbol of man and woman. So I combined the bed with two bodies docked there by the umbilical cord. You don't need a bed, it's just the fact that two people are lying there. Martha wanted a bed—I made a non-bed. The feet were gold—again, trying not to make it a 'bed.' When I had to make a 'woman's place' I made a seat shaped as an hourglass in relation to time. I tried to make a non-seat because I didn't want a chair there. There are many ways of looking at a seat or a bed. The seat is an extension of your spine; the bed is the imperial throne.

"The stepping objects in *Night Journey* are a kind of architecture you walk over. Architecture turns out to be a symbol of imperialism for the conquering hero Oedipus, who is the creator of Athens.

"Martha's contribution is the cloth that comes down, which does succeed in bisecting the space. So you can see, there is more or less a similar thing being accomplished over and over. For Martha, it is a catharsis of her own. She goes through a ritual each time. I was just her assistant with the necessary equipment, like in a hospital.

91

"We are all in a very peculiar dilemma. It's interesting that you should have done a book on Balanchine in relation to his women.[6] I never could figure out what the relationship of Balanchine to women was in the first place. There is something strange. . . . It is not just Balanchine or Martha, it's everybody. Can we be individuals and also a duo? I don't know. It's a very difficult problem. Look at *Night Journey:* There is this ambiguous creature, Jocasta, who was the queen, a lover, and mother —out of that incestuous situation comes the birth of Athens. I find Oedipus at Colonus a fantastic beauty, a requiem. I think once both men and women begin to release their resistance, our relationships will become much more constructive."

NOTES

Noguchi wrote of this set, "Incest. I created a bed, raised on legs of gold, as the central sculpture, a double image of male and female. The approach to this is like fragments of archaeology, the spirits of his ancestors, over whom Oedipus must mount. The chair is Jocasta's place as woman in the shape of an hourglass. Truth is the staff of Teresias, 'who was for seven years a woman.' 'The umbilical cord is a white gleaming thing that links man and woman who love each other.'"

FROM THE ORIGINAL PROGRAM NOTES

"And loudly o'er the bed she wailed where she
In twofold wedlock, hapless, had brought forth
Husband from a husband, children from a child.
We could not know the moment of her death
Which followed soon."
—Sophocles

"In Greek mythology, Oedipus is the hero who killed his father and married his mother. He was the son of King Laius of Thebes and Jocasta, the Queen. At his birth, an oracle declared that he would murder his father and he was, therefore, abandoned on a desolate mountainside. He was found by a Corinthian shepherd, was protected, and grew to manhood as the adopted son of the King of Corinth. Again an oracle predicted that he would slay his father and marry his mother. Thinking the King of Corinth his true father, he fled the city and in his wanderings met, quarreled with, and killed a stranger who was King Laius of Thebes. He went to Thebes, solved the riddle of the Sphinx and as a consequence became a King and married the Queen, Jocasta. He was a noble king and reigned happily until a plague ravaged Thebes and the oracle declared that only the banishment of the murderer of Laius would relieve the city. The terrible truth of his fate was brought to light by the seer Tiresias. Jocasta took her own life; Oedipus blinded himself and wandered the earth in misery.

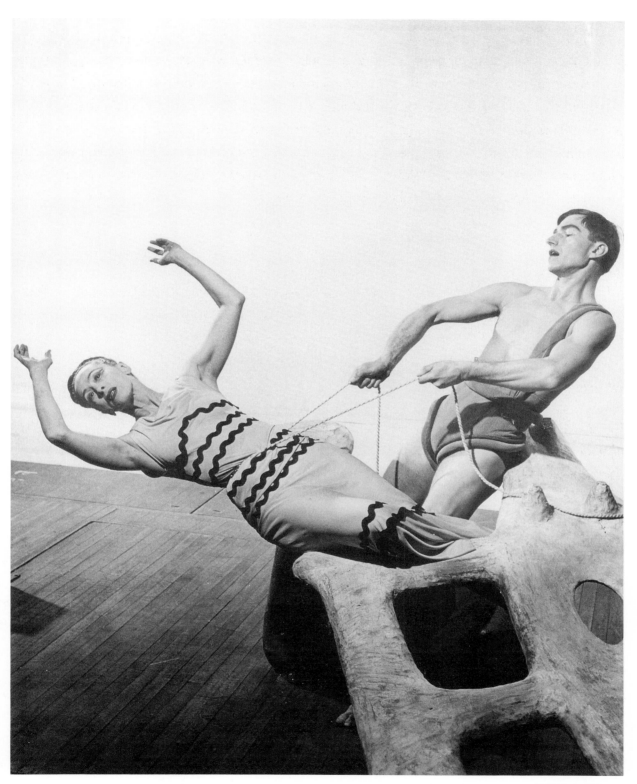

© Arnold Eagle

© Arnold Eagle

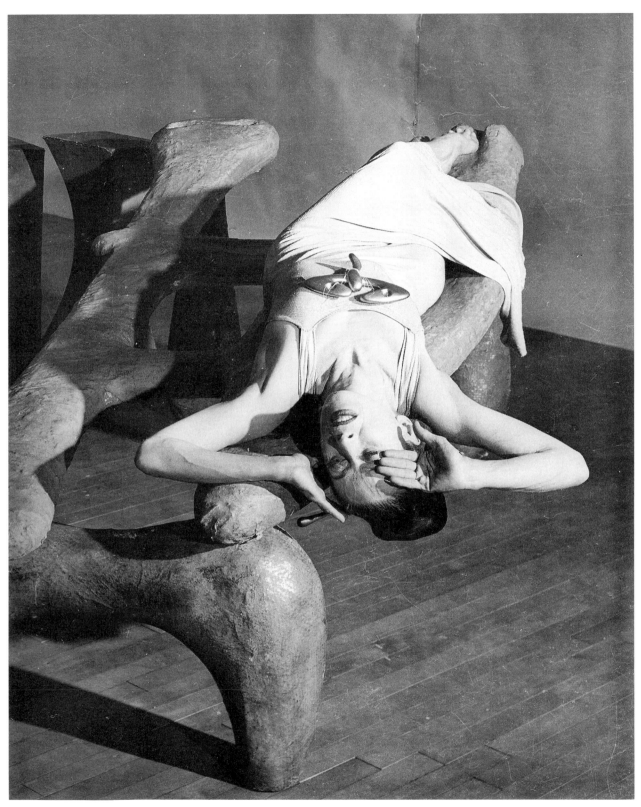

"*In* Night Journey, *Martha Graham's dramatization of this great myth, it is not Oedipus but the Queen Jocasta who is the protagonist. The action of the dance turns upon that instant of her death when she relives her destiny, sees with double insight the triumphal entry of Oedipus, their meeting, courtship, marriage, their years of intimacy which were darkly crossed by the blind seer Tiresias until at last the truth burst from him. The chorus of women who know the truth before the seer speaks it try in vain to divert the prophecy from its cruel conclusion."*

FROM ANOTHER VERSION

"This dance is a legend of recognition. The action takes place in Jocasta's heart at the moment when she recognizes the ultimate terms of her destiny. She enters her room where the precise fulfillment of its terms awaits her. Here the Daughters of Night, Oedipus in his inescapable role, and the Seer pursue themselves across her heart in that instant of agony."

THE SEASONS

Choreography by Merce Cunningham
Music by John Cage
Set by Isamu Noguchi
Costumes by Isamu Noguchi

Premiered May 18, 1947
Ziegfeld Theatre, New York
Performed by Balanchine and Kirstein's Ballet Society

"Lincoln [Kirstein] may have asked me to design *The Seasons* for Ballet Society. I knew Lincoln from when I first did his head in the late 1920s. I'm rather disappointed that they never did *The Seasons* again. They say they can't find the parts, but they could also re-create it. Merce and John have their own trajectory, and it probably doesn't fit into the plan. They don't like to go back and show their beginnings—maybe because their beginnings go back to Martha. I liked the development of *The Seasons* and what I was able to do. It is more a commentary on my own contribution. It had meaning and it flowed. It was a passage of time which showed like seasons.

"It started with nothing: no light, just blackness. Merce was sitting with his back to the audience. One very vaguely sees him as the lights come up slowly, and everything slowly comes to life, and it becomes like dawn. These birds come in with tail feathers and red beaks held in their mouths. There is a dance of early spring. I had a lot of projections and flashes of magnesium which didn't seem to distract. When the sun comes in—on a wheel which has a tangle of rods—I used a projection of fire in the background. And then there is autumn and winter that follow. A man comes out with a beehive stuck on his leg and a mask on his face. He is very tall, gray, and lonely, walking through the snow like doom. In the back there is a stretching of a cat's cradle with ropes. It was very simple and seemed to gel. It flowed and crystallized the space. It is a whole world-whole time cycle—a man's epic. It was a big theme. It was done three times and that was the end of that.

"The costumes I designed were like Mack Sennett's costumes. They were very funny-looking. They were comic and sad, much like the human condition."

NOTES

Noguchi wrote, "I saw The Seasons *as a celebration of the passage of time. The time could be either a day, from dawn through the heat of midday to the cold of night, or a year, as the title suggests, or a life-time.*

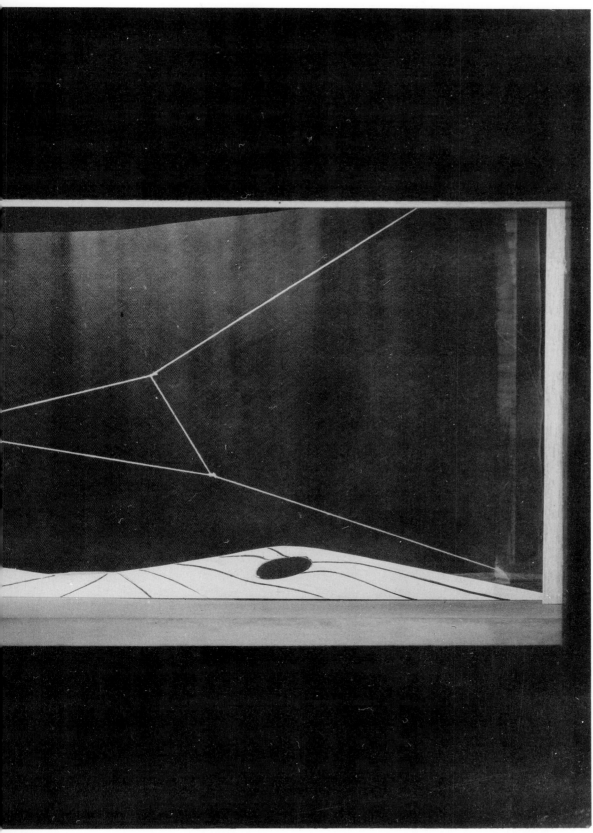

"In the beginning there is darkness or nothingness (before consciousness). It is raining as the light grows to bare visibility, to die, and then to revive again, pulsating and growing ever stronger.

"Suddenly in a flash (magnesium flash), it is dawn. (All this is done with light machines). Birds (beaks for boys, tail feathers for girls) dance to the morning.

"The light becomes hotter, the throbbing heat becomes intense, until with violence it bursts into flames (light projections throughout).

"Autumn follows, with strange, soft moon shapes, then the cold of winter. It is snowing; lines of freezing ice transfix the sky (ropes), and the man of doom walks into the dark.

"Although The Seasons was presented only three times, I have always felt it to be one of my best contributions. The costumes—somewhat like Mack Sennett bathing costumes, like birds with and without tail feathers. The beaks of red cellophane cones, mounted on white circular disks, were held in the dancer's teeth."

FROM THE ORIGINAL PROGRAM NOTES

"The ballet is divided into the four seasons commencing with Winter. Each Season is preceded by a prelude. The curtain rises on the first prelude which is orchestral. The dance action commences with Winter. With regard to The Seasons, Mr. Cunningham says:

"I have tried to use the materials of myth, that is, the wending of a span of nature's time, in my own terms. And if time and the seasons are inseparable, it seems to me that time and dancing are hardly less so. The preludes that announce each season, attempt to catch moments that might exist in a life, or in any fraction of human time."

"John Cage, composer of The Seasons, writes of his work:

"The scenario given me by Mr. Cunningham was the basis for a study of numbers with which I find it congenial to begin a musical composition. His remark, "the fullness and stillness of a summer day," suggested that Summer would be the longest section; that, together with his desire that each would be developed by continuous invention and preceded by a short formal prelude (formal by means of exact repetitions), and that the entire work would be cyclical and concise, brought about the following numerical situation: 2,2; 1,3; 2,4; 1,3; 1. The number, 4, represents Summer, since it is the largest number (it is also the smallest number which could be the largest number in this situation); the first 3 is Spring, the second, Fall (3's are, like these seasons, assymetrical, un-static); they suggest both the approach to and away from 4. The second 2 is Winter, for 2 suggests the place between two 3's, opposite a 4. The other numbers are the Preludes. Summer (4) has a Prelude of 2 (fittingly, the longest), Spring and Fall have Preludes of 1. Winter has a Prelude of 2 which is actually 1 repeated.

"This was done to provide an instrumental description of atmosphere before the actual dancing begins (the ballet begins with Winter), and to provide an end-piece which was the same, but suitably proportioned *to the other preludes as dance accompaniment. This made 2 to begin with and 1 to end with. The entire series of numbers occurs throughout the ballet, not only with respect to the length of sections, but, as is my custom in works for percussion and "prepared" piano, also with respect to phraseology. Thus within each 1, the series given above occurs as the determinant of breathing. Within the 4 of Summer, it occurs 4 times, etc. The tempo changes the actual number of measures as it changes: actual time length being the basis of this plan. Naturally, a plan like this is made not only to be followed, but also that it may be broken. Yet the pleasure of breaking a law can only exist if the law is existent. The question arises whether one can know this rhythmic structure from a first hearing. The answer clearly is: No."*

TALE OF SEIZURE

Choreography by Yuriko
Music by Louis Horst
Set by Isamu Noguchi
Costume by Yuriko

Premiered February 17-29, 1948
Maxine Elliott Theatre, New York
Performed by Yuriko

"For Yuriko, I had these cones of light made of plastic that just sit on the floor around the stage. Yuriko danced through these lighted objects, and there was another light object which had projection on it from behind. In fact, it was self-illuminating. There was not very much light, excepting these luminous objects Yuriko danced among. I was using light as part of the set, as a matter of fact."

NOTES

Said Yuriko, "The dance was leading myself away to light in order to embark on my own ancestral roots."

A 1949 Dance Observer *review of* Tale of Seizure *at a YM-YWHA concert stated, "We do, however, take exception to the Noguchi set for* Tale of Seizure *because it becomes too important and arouses associated patterns which conflict the idea of this dance with two of Martha Graham's works." [7]*

ORPHEUS

Choreography by George Balanchine
Music by Igor Stravinsky
Set by Isamu Noguchi
Costumes by Isamu Noguchi

Premiered April 28, 1948
City Center of Music and Drama, New York
Performed by Balanchine's and Kirstein's Ballet Society
Revived by the New York City Ballet in 1972 and again in 1979 for Mikhail Baryshnikov

"Orpheus was a very personal involvement on my part. The feeling was shared by Balanchine, Stravinsky, and everybody who had anything to do with it. It remained as kind of testament to the artist. It still is. In that case too, these rocks that are lying on the earth come to life and rise up. That, by the way, was my definition of how mortals descend into the netherworld. These rising rocks make them go down, relatively speaking.

"The figure of Orpheus and the figure of Death descending into another world is a kind of passage which I believe was enhanced enormously by Balanchine's white, billowing curtain. I did not do the curtain, so there is no reason accusing me of having done the curtain. I know I didn't do it. I believe it was Balanchine because he had done it before with Pavel Tchelitchew in *Errante* [created for Les Ballets 1933 in Paris], where the silk was up near the ceiling, floating around like clouds. It floated up there, it was not used as a physical part of the action. Balanchine took it and used it, and he made a lot of people very angry. Tchelitchew thought I stole it. I didn't steal it, it wasn't me.

"From my own point of view, I was very involved with the myth. I related it to the Japanese myth of Izanagi-No-Mikoto [and] Izanami-No-Mikoto, the two gods who are married and one dies and the other goes to fetch her [from the underworld].[8] He almost gets her out when he makes the mistake of looking back to see what she is like, and she is full of worms. He shrieks and tries to get out as fast as possible. He gets out of the hole and slams this enormous rock into the spot so she can't follow him. After he is out in the world she says, 'What have you done to me? I will slay someone.' That is the Japanese myth I used to create Orpheus. Orpheus does not see that Eurydice is dead because he is blind. The idea of her is much stronger than any reality he might have seen.

"The mask for Orpheus probably comes from Japan, too. In common folk dances one finds the use of the towel, tenugui, which is used all kinds of ways—wrapped around the head, stuck into the mouth. If one is about to become a thief one uses it to disguise oneself. You see, I have a repertoire that comes from my childhood in Japan.

"It is very interesting to compare both Balanchine and Martha. The ballet started with representational, recognizable elements. With Balanchine, the early years were full of clothes and recognizable elements of costume. Gradually, it became just the body. He dispensed with costumes almost entirely. It was an encumbrance. Martha never divested herself of clothes. With Martha, costumes did not play a part in embracing her emotional ambiance: They did not create it, they were just costumes. Martha never allowed me to do a costume for her. She did not trust me. She was afraid I would not be able to give her the kind of attractiveness which she particularly wanted and which she required.

"I never thought of myself as a costume designer. I was not too confident about those things. I don't think I was competent along those lines. I've done a few, like Balanchine's *Orpheus* and *King Lear* for Gielgud. Those were exceptions and also strenuous for me. On the other hand, I enjoyed designing them enormously for the theater."

NOTES

Noguchi wrote, "Never was I more personally involved in creation than with this piece which is the story of the artist. I interpreted Orpheus *as the story of the artist blinded by his vision (the mask). Even inanimate objects move at his touch—as do the rocks, at the pluck of his lyre. To find his bride or to seek his dream or to fulfill his mission, he is drawn by the spirit of darkness to the netherworld. He descends in gloom as glowing rocks, like astral bodies, levitate: and as he enters Hades, from behind a wildly floating silk curtain the spirits of the dead emerge. Here, too, entranced by his art, all obey him; and even Pluto's rock turns to reveal Eurydice in his embrace.*

"With his music Orpheus, who is blinded to all material facts by the mask of his art, leads Eurydice earthward. But, alas, he is now beset by doubts of material possession. He tears off his mask and sees Eurydice as she really is, a creature of death. Without the protection of his artistic powers, he is even weaker than ordinary mortals, and he is torn apart by the Furies. But his art is not dead; his singing head has grown heroic as his spirit returns; and as a symbol of this resurrection, a flowering branch ascends to heaven."

FROM THE ORIGINAL PROGRAM NOTES

"According to Greek mythology, Orpheus, grief-stricken over the death of Eurydice, his wife, is led by his Dark Angel undergound into Hades where the music of his lyre quiets the Furies, consoles the Lost Souls and finally charms Pluto into returning Eurydice to him, exacting from him the promise not to look at her

111

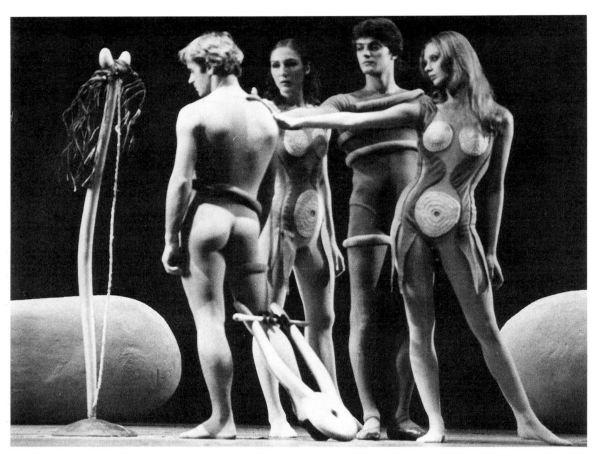

© Carolyn George

© Carolyn George

until they reach the upper air. He begins his tortured journey earthward, blindfolded, with Eurydice at whom he must not look. She, unknowing, persuades him to tear the mask from his eyes, thereby bringing about her instant and irrevocable death. Back on earth, Orpheus is torn to pieces by the Bacchantes, the women of Thrace whom he, lost in his inconsolable grief, has treated with contempt. The ballet ends as Apollo invokes the spirit of Orpheus as the God of Song."

REVIVAL PROGRAM NOTES

"When Igor Stravinsky was commissioned by Ballet Society, Inc. to write Orpheus, the subject chosen by Balanchine, composer and choreographer worked closely with each other on every aspect of the work. The distinguished sculptor Isamu Noguchi designed the scenery, objects and costumes.

"Orpheus, which led the late Morton Baum to invite Ballet Society to become the New York City Ballet, with residency at the City Center, remained in the repertory until 1964 just before the company moved, under the aegis of City Center, to the New York State Theatre. Noguchi has rescaled and renewed his work for this revival."

WILDERNESS STAIR (DIVERSION OF ANGELS)

(Original title Wilderness Stair, *from a poem by Ben Belitt; first performance only)*
Choreography by Martha Graham
Music by Norman Dello Joio
Set by Isamu Noguchi
Costumes by Martha Graham

Premiered August 13, 1948
Palmer Auditorium, Connecticut College, New London, Connecticut
Performed by the Martha Graham Company

"This was the dance I did the backdrop for the stage. I tried to manipulate the back curtain in a way to make a landscape, by having the backdrop made out of burlap where I was able to push things through the curtain. I was manipulating it through shadow. I cast a light sideways and one is able to see this landscape transforming itself like a desert landscape. [It was an image of breasts and valleys.] We did the dance up at Connecticut. It didn't seem to work out quite right. It was a distraction, as often happens when one tries to have an interest which is in itself too interesting, and created in the end it is a distraction. It was an original concept without being based on experience. I think Martha also felt that way about it."

NOTES

This set was eliminated after the first performance.

Noguchi wrote, "When this dance was first presented at Connecticut College I devised a full burlap backdrop, stretched along all its edges by ropes through grommets. From behind, here and there, long rods were pushed to modulate the cloth into undulating clouds of breasts and valleys. Unfortunately this was considered too distracting for the dance, and so was dropped."

FROM THE ORIGINAL PROGRAM NOTES

Originally entitled Wilderness Stair, *after a poem by Ben Belitt, This dance follows no story. Its action takes place in the imaginary garden love creates for itself. Belitt wrote, 'It is the place of the Rock and the Ladder, the raven, the blessing, the tempter, the rose. It is the wish of the single-hearted, the undivided: play after spirit's labor: games, flights, fancies, configurations of the lover's intentions: the believed Possibility, at once strenuous and tender: humour of innocence, garland, evangels, Joy on the wilderness stair, diversion of angels.'*

FROM THE LATTER VERSION

The dance was renamed Diversion of Angels, whose program note included a quote from Thomas Traherne:

"The city seemed to stand in Eden or to be built in Heaven...The dust and stones of the streets were as precious as gold...Eternity was manifested in the light of day and something infinite beyond everything appeared, which talked with my expectation and moved my desire...The Men! Immortal Cherubim! And young men glittering, and sparkling angels, and maids seraphic pieces of life and beauty. Boys and girls tumbling in the streets and playing, were moving jewels. I knew not that they were born or should die...The streets were mine...the temple was mine, their clothes and gold and silver were mine, and so were the sun and moon and stars, and all the world was mine, and I the only spectator and enjoyer of it.

"The dance was called 'a lyric dance about the loveliness of youth, the pleasure and playfulness, quick joy and quick sadness of being in love for the first time.'"

JUDITH

Choreography by Martha Graham
Music by William Schuman
Set by Isamu Noguchi
Costume by Martha Graham
Headdress, cuffs and collar by Isamu Noguchi

Premiered January 4, 1950
Columbia Auditorium, Louisville, Kentucky
Performed by Martha Graham

"I don't like scrims because they are a trick. With the experience of the New York City premiere of *Judith* at Carnegie Hall, I had to use something to disguise the orchestra onstage, so I used scrims. Then we were invited to Berlin to perform in the Kongresshalle, and I was hesitant because also over there they had an orchestra and there was no way of hiding the damn thing. So I took the scrims I used in Carnegie Hall and changed them into fishnets. I got someone to weave me some very rough fishnet which I put on these frames. The space seemed to work much better because it was defined. The areas of the stage were defined by a bunch of disguises, or distractions, of the orchestra. Instead of seeing the orchestra, one's eye was stopped by what was on the scrim—these cutout clothes. The images on the fishnets were just any old thing. It seemed to work, to my satisfaction, given the circumstances in Berlin. Martha continually used them for a while but then she abandoned them for the objects like Holofernes's tent and 'the woman's place.'

"Holofernes's tent is this fluid object which the audience appreciates, and Martha often uses cloth as an additional visual titillation. That is Martha for you. Her use of props is performed like a bit of magic. I don't know if anyone else can do it like she did."

NOTES

Noguchi wrote, "I carved the tent of Holofernes out of balsa wood in the shape of an animal (stage left); Judith's place as a lyre or a loom (stage right). Between these two the action takes place.

"This was presented in Carnegie Hall before the Louisville Symphony Orchestra, for which it was commissioned. With the large orchestra in full view there was only a narrow space to dance in.

"The problem was how to distract the audience's consciousness away from the orchestra. To hide it, as we attempted with a scrim in Carnegie Hall, was unsatisfactory (I dislike the ambiguous quality of scrim).

However, I was later given another chance to resolve this problem upon the occasion of the opening of Kongresshalle in Berlin (September 1957), when there was no means even to hang a scrim. I therefore devised a way of camouflaging the orchestra by superimposing an even greater distraction between it and the dancer. White cloth shapes were sewed on stands of fishnet, so that the audience was effectively blinded from seeing the orchestra and their light stands."

He continued, using the words of Martha Graham,"The story of Judith is a fertility rite, that involves the releasing of the waters. When death is overcome or obviated, then she emerges with white flowing branches— after a tragedy to accept life, to shed the garments of sadness, to put on those of gladness."

FROM THE ORIGINAL PROGRAM NOTES

"The story of Judith is part of the Apocryphal writings. It tells

"Of how…'Holofernes took the waters and the fountains of waters of the children of Israel…therefore, their young children were out of heart and their women and young men fainted of thirst…and there was no longer any strength in them…and they were brought very low in the city…'

"Of how…'Judith fell upon her face…and cried with loud voice and said…"O Lord God of my father Simeon to whom thou gavest a sword to take vengeance of the strangers…

Give into mine hand the…power I have conceived…

Smite them by the deceit of my lips…

Break down their statelines by the hand of a woman.

Lord God of the Heavens and Earth

Creator of the waters…

Hear my prayer." '

"Of how…'Judith put off the garments of her widowhood for the exaltation of those that were oppressed.' and

'Put on her garments of gladness' and went 'down the mountain…to the tent of Holofernes…'

"Of how…'She abode in the camp three days…and she besought the Lord God to direct her way…'

"Of how…'On the fourth day Holofernes made a feast…

When Judith came in and sat down, Holofernes in his heart was ravished with her…and he drank more wine than he had drunk at any one day since he was born…'

"Of how…'When evening came his servants made haste to depart…and Judith was left alone in the tent and Holofernes lying along his bed for he was filled with wine…'

"Of how…'Judith standing by his bed said in her heart: "O Lord God of all power…strenghthen me this day…" '

"Of how…'She took his head from him…and went forth up the mountain

…and said with a loud voice:

"Behold the head of Holofernes…the Lord has smitten him by the hand of a woman…I will sing unto the Lord a new song."'

"Of how…'The women…made a dance among them for her…and she took branches in her hand…and she went before all the people in the dance.'"

VOYAGE

Choreography by Martha Graham
Music by William Schuman
Set by Isamu Noguchi
Costumes by Edythe Gilfond

Premiered May 17, 1953
Alvin Theatre, New York
Performed by Martha Graham and Company

"Martha wanted to do a dance on the poem, 'Anabasis,' an Arabian allegory by St. John Perse. Actually, I met Perse with Martha. Stokowski was to do the music. It had to do with a caravan in the desert. So I made a sail and a boat, which is quite incongruous, but being asked to do a voyage, well, it was easier for me to do something with a boat than with camels. She originally wanted something she could dance in, in very formal attire—'black tie,' so to speak. I don't know why she wanted that, but she did. It was a preconception. How do you figure out this very formal attire in relation to a sail and a boat? I don't know. It was quite logical it should become *Circe* [in 1963] and not stay *Anabasis,* which was the original title."

NOTES

Noguchi wrote, "Based on the poem 'Anabasis' by St. John Perse which deals with migration to a new land in terms of an Arabian allegory.

"Why I did a boat and sail for a desert caravan I do not know. Obviously, the set seemed made for something else. By strange inevitability and the genius of Miss Graham the same set was reused ten years later for an entirely different theme in Circe.*"*

Bertram Ross said in an interview with the author that Martha Graham originally wanted a porch on which she would be able to walk in order to separate herself from a very sophisticated formal party. The porch would enable her to look out on a great plain or a huge desert—infinity. Noguchi's design was of a vagina illuminated with little red lights when the three men walked through it. Notes Ross, "There were even pubic hairs. Martha said to Noguchi, 'You are very naughty.'"[9]

The sail and the boat were Noguchi's final design, the huge desert landscape having been changed to an enormous seascape through which the dancers could walk.

"This dance is a theatre for four characters voyaging on the strange seas of intimacy, caught in the ebb and flow, the tragic and comic cross-currents of relationships."

THEATER OF A VOYAGE

Choreography by Martha Graham
Music by William Schuman
Set by Isamu Noguchi
Costumes by Edythe Gilfond

Premiered May 5, 1955
ANTA Theatre, New York
Performed by Martha Graham and Company

NOTES

The original piano score for Voyage (1953) was orchestrated for the re-working of this dance. Bertram Ross explained in an interview with the author that Martha Graham tried three times to solve the choreographic problems of this dance. "In Theater of a Voyage, the dancers performed in summer clothes. Martha had on a halter top with a bare midriff—a brassiere— and a short skirt to her knee," he said. "She only wore this costume once. She immediately changed back to a black dress. She wore her hair down and the three men would put things into her hair and then take them out."

"In Voyage," Ross continued, "Martha made no choices in terms of her relationships with the three men [played by Bertram Ross, Robert Cohan and Stuart Hodes]. At the end of the dance everyone went his own merry way to avoid colliding with anyone, so new possibilities could come. It was a non-sexual confrontation—no romance. Martha just wanted to work after Erick [Hawkins] had left and divorced her. However, in Theater of a Voyage, two year later, she ended up with me as her sexual partner and left Bob and Stuart behind. We then went on a romantic journey."

"The third version," he added, "which never got produced, was the most mysterious. Martha was determined to make this dance work because the reviewers always thought the dance was a failure."[10]

FROM THE ORIGINAL PROGRAM NOTES

"…And let the sadness that was ours be dissolved again in the wine of men.

To it we lift a new face, in it we wash a new face

Covenanters and witnesses take oath before the fonts

And should the face of any man near us fail

to do honor to life, let that face be held

by force into wind.

© Arnold Eagle

The gods who walk in the wind do not raise the whip in vain.
O Thou, desire who are about to sing."

—St. John Perse

SERAPHIC DIALOGUE

Choreography by Martha Graham
Music by Norman Dello Joio
Set by Isamu Noguchi
Costumes by Martha Graham

Premiered May 8, 1955
ANTA Theatre, New York
Performed by the Martha Graham Company

"I perceived the whole action [of Joan of Arc] taking place in front of a cathedral, but how was I to put a cathedral there? I asked my friend Edison Price to help me with that. I did the structural part of the props and Edison did the structural part of the cathedral. I thought the cathedral could be held up with these wires through brass rods which had knuckle joints and therefore allowed it to collapse, in the same way as Ruth Page's *The Bells.* As I've said, it is from *The Bells* that I got *Seraphic Dialogue.* They were both churches. In the case of Joan of Arc [*Seraphic Dialogue*], a collapse does not take place like it did in *The Bells.* In *Seraphic Dialogue,* it is a permeating thing which the dancers can go in and out of. They can even move sections. It is very fluid and seems to work beautifully."

NOTES

Noguchi wrote, "I depicted the life of Joan of Arc as a cathedral that fills her consciousness entirely. To do this, I constructed a transparent edifice of brass tubing—articulated like a church steeple, as I had done for The Bells, *a ballet in 1944 for the Ballet Russe de Monte Carlo, but with a different purpose. The construction was a precision operation, made possible by my friend, Edison Price."*

"It is like all cathedrals, but also like no cathedral on earth, more like the golden lines which for us is a cathedral, whether the lines of the arches or the arches made by the light of candles and gold."—Martha Graham

FROM THE ORIGINAL PROGRAM NOTES

"The title of the work about Joan of Arc is from St. Catherine of Sienna.

"Joan of Arc, heroine of France, was born in the village of Domremy in 1412, the child of peasants. While still a girl, she became a military leader, raised the English seige of Orleans in 1429, and crowned

© Arnold Eagle

the Dauphin Charles VII. Shortly afterward, she was captured by the English and, after a long terrible trial, she was burned at the stake as a witch. She was declared a saint by the Roman Catholic Church in 1920. *Seraphic Dialogue* is a drama about Joan of Arc."

FROM LATER PROGRAM NOTES

"Seraphic Dialogue *is a drama about Joan of Arc at the moment of her exaltation. In a dialogue with Saint Michael, Saint Catherine, and Saint Margaret, whose voices had guided her toward her destiny, she looks back upon herself as a maiden, a warrior, and a martyr. She is then taken up to her place of honor.*"

CLYTEMNESTRA

Choreography by Martha Graham
Music by Halim El-Dabh
Set by Isamu Noguchi
Costumes by Martha Graham and Helen McGehee

Premiered April 1, 1958
Adelphi Theatre, New York
Performed by Martha Graham and Company

"Martha's 'Americana period' was influenced maybe by the American Indian, and the 'epic period' by a mythological context, although I am sure that the American Indian is 'mythological.' With Martha, the Greek legends had the creative something in them which set her off. Mythology is a language; mythology became her language. Martha never thought of making a 'Greek cycle'. She would diverge. At the same time she would choreograph *Every Soul Is a Circus* (1939), something like that, or *Appalachian Spring* (1944) or *Hérodiade* (1944). She just happened to do something on a myth—one thing led to the next.

"In 1958, she did *Clytemnestra* and *Embattled Garden*: one is Greek, the other, biblical. She is interested in the realm of myth, whether it's Greek or Hebraic really doesn't matter that much. It's the land of dream which Martha was able to capture. It's a kind of 'mindscape'—that's a very good word, like 'landscape.' I'm very much interested in landscape. But with Martha it probably is 'mindscape' more than 'landscape.'

"By *Clytemnestra* though, Martha was on her own, and all that was left were the props. But even the props were also very ephemeral by then. They were starting to disappear. You see, then Martha was free to do it her own way without any assistance. I was disappearing like a Cheshire Cat. What I'm trying to say is she was taking over, I was gradually disappearing. She may have needed me at some point, but by the time of *Clytemnestra* we were beginning to grow apart. I personally don't feel involved unless I'm really necessary—really a collaborator. In a way, Martha could get a piece of cloth and whirl it around and it would serve her a purpose. I was merely supplying her with rudimentary props.

"In *Clytemnestra* there is a curtain which flies in from above. It is the cloak of Agamemnon—the golden cloak. I did various things like that. I did elements of the other props but she combined them into her own way. The way she moves things around and combines them is extraordinary. I also made the seat, of course, 'the woman's place.' "

Noguchi wrote, *"A dance of retribution after death. Out of the dark unconscious comes memory —the terrible devastation 'when the war spears clashed in Troy.' The unencumbered stage. Space is isolated only by props which focus the eye of the imagination. Crossed spears, the throne of Knossos, the golden cloak of Agamemnon fills the sky. Continuous change covering forty-five minutes."*

FROM THE ORIGINAL PROGRAM NOTES

"Denied honor among the dead, Clytemnestra asks the question we ask in face of punishment: Why?

"…Because she asks the question of her Furies, her inner self, Clytemnestra has set the machinery of reply in motion.

"…Throughout the dance, the image of the net recurs as it does in all tragedy. Each small act serves to draw the net tighter. It means complete death unless there is some act of rebirth, a subjugation of the will to the forces of spirit.

"…The action is performed within the dangerous landscape of the mind…and there is no limit to the drama the mind can evoke."

Excerpts from the script of Clytemnestra *by Martha Graham:*

"The Action:

"The prologue begins with Clytemnestra reweaving in her memory the net of her doom. She stands dishonoured before Hades, King of the Dead, struggling to understand her past—her murder of her husband Agamemnon, newly returned from the Trojan Wars with his captive, the seer Cassandra—and her fate. The appearance of her sister, Helen of Troy, evokes in Clytemnestra the vision of the Rape of Troy, the sacrifice of her daughter Iphigenia by Agamemnon to appease the gods, and the meeting of her children, Electra and Orestes, to plot her death. They seek revenge for the slaying of their father, Agamemnon, by Clytemnestra, who was urged on in consort while Agamemnon warred in Troy.

"Clytemnestra and Helen of Troy were sisters, the daughters, according to a legend, of Leda and Zeus. They married brothers, Agamemnon and Menelaus, the sons of King Atreus of Mycenae. Helen, who had 'terribly the look, close up, of the immortal goddesses…' was seduced by Paris and carried away to Troy. Agamemnon and Menelaus drained Greece of its manhood in raising the armies that would sail to Troy to win her back; Clytemnestra was left alone in Mycenae, in a palace itself drained of men. 'It is evil and a thing of terror,' she said, 'when a wife sits in the house forlorn with no man by.' But it was her sister Helen, not she, who sat forlorn, idle in Troy. Clytemnestra ruled Mycenae; with her 'male strength of heart,' she was both King and Queen to the state, both father and mother to her children.

"Evil and things of terror came quickly. The great armies gathered at Aulis, ready to sail for the Trojan War, were stopped by storms. Agamemnon was told by a prophet that he was the cause: he had offended

the goddess Artemis and the weather would not break until he had offered a suitable sacrifice. Agamemnon sent messengers back to Mycenae to tell Clytemnestra that he had arranged a marriage betweeen Achilles, the greatest of the Greek heroes, and their daughter, Iphigenia. Clytemnestra prepared Iphigenia ('my love, my flower of pain,' she called her) for this great wedding and sent her to Aulis and there Agamemnon took her and sacrificed her to the goddess. The weather broke, the fleet sailed and the Trojan War began.

"For revenge, Clytemnestra would have killed her young son, Agamemnon's beloved Orestes, but the boy was saved by Electra, his sister, who sent him away into hiding on Mount Parnassus. Clytemnestra ruled like a man, took a lover, the 'womanish' Aegisthus, who was Agamemnon's cousin and blood-enemy, waited and plotted.

"Beacon fires, lighted across the face of the ancient world, announced the fall and destruction of Troy. Clytemnestra described it all to the people of Mycenae in an ecstatic vision. Agamemnon, arrogant in his triumph, returned, bringing with him his captive and mistress, Cassandra, the royal princess of Troy, who had the gift of infallible prophecy and the curse that no one who heard her would believe. Clytemnestra received them with great pomp, spread for Agamemnon a gorgeous robe to walk upon and led him into the palace and killed him. Cassandra shrieked her prophecy of his death and of her own but none of the people believed. She went after Agamemnon into the palace and it was not long before Clytemnestra reappeared, declaring herself a murderess but 'a righteous craftsman.' She defied the people of Mycenae, married Aegisthus and continued her rule, thinking that, since her own lust for vengeance had been satisfied, no more evil would be done.

"But that lust had passed to her daughter, Electra. As Clytemnestra had waitied for Agamemnon, Electra waited for her brother, Orestes.

"Orestes, grown to manhood, returned to Mycenae disguised as a traveller, revealed himself to Electra and together they plotted revenge for their father's death. As Clytemnestra, with the help of Aegisthus, had murdered Agamemnon and Cassandra, Orestes, with Electra's help, murdered Aegisthus and Clytemnestra.

"The lust for vengeance passed back again to Clytemnestra. From the kingdom of the dead, from 'that most deep and subterranean end of wandering,' where of all the Greeks she alone went dishounoured, Clytemnestra pursued Orestes, set the Furies, 'his mother's wrathful hounds,' upon him and drove him mad. She would have destroyed him if it had not been for a great trial that took place on the rock of Athens in which Orestes, as accused, and the Furies, as accusers, submitted the case to an Athenian jury and to Athena herself. The goddess, in casting the deciding vote in Orestes' favor, put an end to the evil and things of terror. She ripped apart the terrible net of murder and vengeance, of love-in-hate and hate-in-love, the weaving of which had begun in the ancestral past and which Clytemnestra and Helen and Agamemnon had themselves woven to such a length that it snared all of Greece and Troy and virtually destroyed both. Athena freed Orestes of the blood-curse and transformed the Furies into the Eumenides, 'the well-wishers,' the conscience of humanity.

"Martha Graham's Clytemnestra *begins in the underworld, that 'most deep and subterranean end of wandering.' Here, in the presence of Hades, King of the Dead, Clytemnestra is dishonoured...but rebellious and , as though by the will of Apollo and Athena, the deities of light and wisdom and ultimate human insight, she begins the supreme effort to understand the past and her fate. Helen of Troy appears, beautiful herald of the terror she caused, and Clytemnestra sees again the vision of the rape of Troy. She sees the sacrifice of Iphigenia, then the fateful scene of Orestes's and Electra's meeting and plotting her death. She and Orestes confront each other and together face, in a torment of memory, all of the figures who were woven through their lives: Helen, Paris, Electra, Aegisthus, Iphigenia, Agamemnon, and finally Cassandra. At the sight of Cassandra, Clytemnestra is again possessed by the lust for vengeance.*

"*In Parts II and III, Clytemnestra relives the actual scenes of her life from the time when, from the rooftops of Mycenae, the Watchman announced the fall of Troy to the moment when, in the dead of night in the palace, her nightmares became reality and she and her lover were murdered by her own son.*

"*The Underworld is again the scene in Part IV. Here Clytemnestra resolves the terrible conflicts of her life and heart.*"

© Arnold Eagle

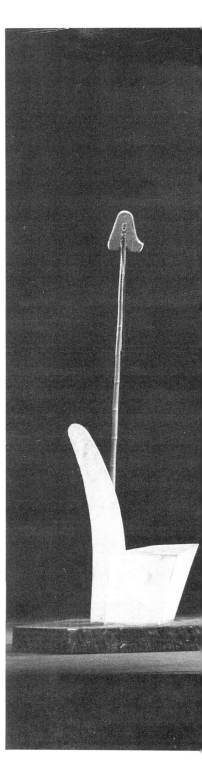

© Sam Frank

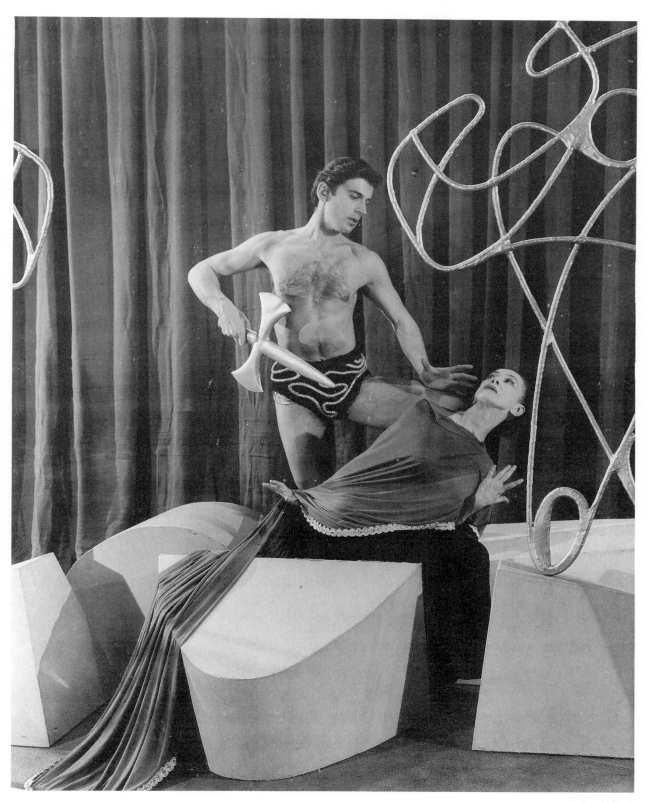

EMBATTLED GARDEN

Choreography by Martha Graham
Music by Carlos Surinach
Set by Isamu Noguchi
Costumes by Martha Graham

Premiered April 3, 1958
Adelphi Theatre, New York
Performed by the Martha Graham Company

"For *Embattled Garden* I used the skin of the apple flattened out, and it is colored like an apple. Worms and worm holes I was able to depict with those rattan rods which stick up and vibrate when [the dancers] dance in the garden. I got the rods in New Jersey. There is a place out there called 'Bamboos and Rattangular.' It is like nature. It is nature's interaction with violence, because some-one is eating the apple. It is a kind of game of appearances, reality, and ideas.

"Sex and violence were what Martha was trying to show. I like that piece very much. My designs are really a reduction of a garden. I make a lot of gardens, and in that way it was almost symbolic. It is like an apple cut in half and the skin is on the inside. One dances within the apple where these weeds are sprouting. They shake. Then there is this tree of knowledge that they climb into. It is the same sprouting. You see the tree I first planted in Martha's *Dark Meadow* (1946), and it sprouted to larger proportions in *Embattled Garden.* I wish I could have the *Embattled Garden* set here at the museum. It would be nice."

NOTES

The Isamu Noguchi Garden Museum does exhibit the apple element, Noguchi's metaphor for Adam and Eve's Garden of Eden, from Embattled Garden.

What was astonishing for 1958 was that Graham created an interracial Garden of Eden *with Yuriko, a Japanese-American, as Eve, and Matt Turney, an African-American, as Lilith. In the early Sixties, Clive Thompson, the great Alvin Ailey dancer who also performed with Graham, said that he danced in an all-black* Garden of Eden *with Mary Hinkson, Matt Turney, and Dudley Williams.*

Noguchi wrote, "The Garden of Eden is the time of puberty. The symbol of the apple was made into a dance platform. Pierced with two large ovals, like the core, but in color patterns like the skin of the apple.

From this rises a jungle of green rattan rods. These vibrate with the dance which takes place between and around them. To the side is the tree."

Noguchi went on to include a quote from Martha Graham, "The Garden of Eden has violence, it is only idyllic now in retrospect."

FROM THE ORIGINAL PROGRAM NOTES

"Love, it has been said, does not obey the rules of love but yields to some more ancient, ruder law. The Garden of Love seems always to be threatened by the Stranger's knowledge of the world outside and by the knowledge of those like Lilith (according to legend, Adam's wife before Eve) who lived there first."

ACROBATS OF GOD

Choreography by Martha Graham
Music by Carlos Surinach
Set by Isamu Noguchi
Costumes by Martha Graham

Premiered April 27, 1960
54th Street Theatre, New York
Performed by Martha Graham and Dance Company

"Martha had occasionally done a piece of a very comic sort but never with sets. So when she asked me to do *Acrobats of God*, I grabbed it. I liked the idea, and I liked the words 'acrobats of God.' It is very acrobatic, with the idea of a dance school or gymnasium. The whole thing has an air of a class taking place—it is a preparation for a performance. Martha couldn't dance by then, so I had her seated there and I had this little sculpture hanging where she could peek around once in a while. In that sense she was still there, and it worked very well. When I saw Peter Brook's *A Midsummer Night's Dream*, it reminded me very much of *Acrobats of God*. It was a set that is not a set. It had the same type of quality—a provisional set."

NOTES

Noguchi called this "a satiric idyll on the instruction of dance. The void of theater space is used three-dimensionally with a huge transfigured practice bar with which, on which, and under which the action takes place. Meaningless symbols float in and out. Martha appears and disappears behind a small, suspended plaque which hides only her face. The music rack of the three mandolin players on stage is also suspended."

FROM THE ORIGINAL PROGRAM NOTES

"To their contemporary biographers, the early church fathers who subjected themselves to the disciplines of the desert were athletae Dei, the athletes of God. This is Martha Graham's fanfare for dance as an art—a celebration in honor of the trials and tribulations, the disciplines, denials, stringencies, glories and delights of a dancer's world...and of the world of the artist."

© Arnold Eagle

© Arnold Eagle

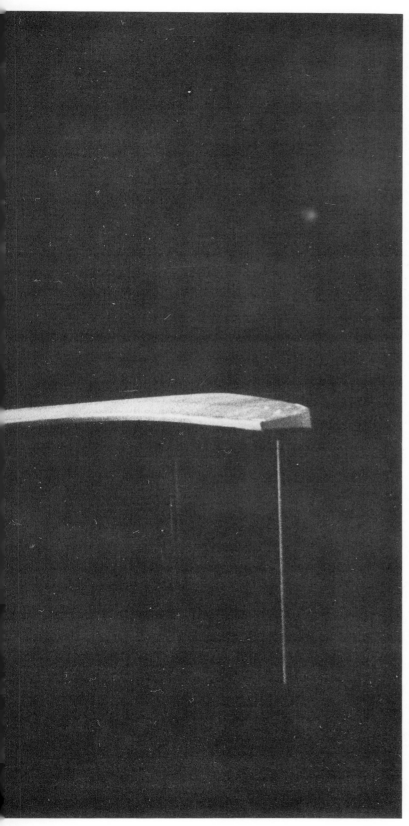

ALCESTIS

Choreography by Martha Graham
Music by Vivian Fine
Set by Isamu Noguchi
Costumes by Martha Graham

Premiered April 29, 1960
54th Street Theatre, New York
Performed by Martha Graham and Dance Company

"You see, these things are not divorced from what I'm doing outside the theater at that particular time. In the case of *Alcestis*, I was designing the garden at Yale University [Beinecke Library]. They are not unfamiliar, they are similar.

"All things become something different when you move them. One thing that contains becomes a liberating force, depending how you use it. It depends upon your point of view. Martha uses the same thing over and over again. I think that's fine if she is inventive.

"In *Alcestis* she wanted a bed. I had made a stone. I might say it's a bed. She used the right angle upside down and rightside up. It became a doorway in *Alcestis*, and in *Phaedra's Dream* (1983), a place for Hippolytus to hang himself."

FROM THE ORIGINAL PROGRAM NOTES
"Alcestis *is a rite of Spring.*

"*The story behind it tells of Admetus and Alcestis who were king and queen in Thessaly. Admetus learned one day that the three Fates had spun all his thread of life and were about to cut it. But he got a respite: if someone could be found to die in his stead, he could live. He went to his parents, his friends, everyone he knew, pleading, but he was refused. Then Alcestis offered to die for him. During the preparations for her funeral, no one was so grief-stricken as Admetus.*

"*In the night of mourning, Hercules arrived at the palace. The standards of hospitality were high in those ancient days and Hercules was royally received and entertained, the news kept from him of the Queen's death. Alcestis was taken to her grave as Hercules ate and drank in his heroic way; when he was reeling*

170

drunk, he heard from a servant what had happened. Ashamed, penitent, to make amends he went to rescue Alcestis, to fight Thanatos, Death himself, and bring her back—and this he did.

"In Martha Graham's dramatization, the myth becomes a festival of the seasons—the death of Winter, the triumphant return of Spring."

PHAEDRA

Choreography by Martha Graham
Music by Robert Starer
Set by Isamu Noguchi
Costumes by Martha Graham

Premiered March 4, 1962
Broadway Theatre, New York
Performed by Martha Graham and Dance Company

"I may have been involved, but only inadvertently did I contribute in that attack by Congress.[11] These were inventions of mine. Martha asked me for a bed, a place for Aphrodite and a place for Hippolytus. Hippolytus appeared in a tall, blue and black, phallic capsule with little doors that opened and revealed various aspects of his anatomy. Aphrodite was in a huge, womb-like sphere which opened to reveal the all but nude goddess tormenting Phaedra. And then the bed. . . . Martha said, 'It slants two ways and you have to lay on it like grim death, or like a greased pig you'll slide off.' It depends how one looks at things. If you didn't have Aphrodite in there with her legs spread apart, it probably wouldn't have occurred to anyone that it was anything but a butterfly. The fact is, I'm not particularly inhibited about sex, and neither is Martha."

NOTES

   Noguchi described the set as "the unenviable bed of lust. The shrine of Aphrodite, like a giant butterfly or womb, opens to reveal the goddess transfixed (stage left). Stage right, the moon goddess Artemis is on her platform. Between them, Phaedra on her golden bed. Stage right rear, Hyppolytus is inside his blue and black horned capsule whose small doors open to reveal his anatomy. He is the cosmonaut weary of this world. The man and the woman's area, right and left, droit versus maladroit, the unknown, sinister. The crossroad of decision."

FROM THE ORIGINAL PROGRAM NOTES

   "Phaedra's father was Minos, King of Crete, and her mother was Pasiphae, she who, cursed by Poseidon, lusted for a bull and conceived the Minotaur. Phaedra's sister was Ariadne, who gave Theseus the secret of the labyrinth and fled with him and was lost on Naxos. Phaedra herself married Theseus in his later years and came as his queen to Athens and there found Hippolytus, his son.

"A great hunter and athlete, worshipper of chaste Artemis, Hippolytus was Theseus's pride…but he was hated by Aphrodite, the Goddess of Love, whom he scorned, and she punished him. As Poseidon had cursed Pasiphae, Aphrodite cursed Phaedra with uncontrollable lust for her husband's son. Hippolytus spurned her, as he would have spurned any woman, and Phaedra, shamed, anguished, desperate, determined to kill herself. Before she died, she wrote a letter to Theseus accusing Hippolytus of having violated her. Theseus, finding her dead, finding the letter, drove his son out and cursed him. Hippolytus, fleeing, was killed and then Theseus learned the truth.

"Martha Graham's Phaedra is focused upon that time outside of time when, at the pitch of her lust, Phaedra chooses the lie, sees it as reality and sees its consequences even as, in a nightmare vision of the past and of Pasiphae's lust, she understands her own lust and tragedy."

FROM ANOTHER VERSION

"The supernatural power behind the human action in the Greek myth is portrayed by the two goddesses, Artemis, the chaste one, and Aphrodite, the Cyprian, the unconquerable goddess of love and lust.

"Phaedra, in her obsession for her stepson, Hippolytus, is the victim of this power, which used her to enact the lie which brings destruction of the House."

© Nan Melville

CIRCE

Choreography by Martha Graham
Music by Alan Hovhaness
Set by Isamu Noguchi
Costumes by Martha Graham

Premiered September 6, 1963
Prince of Wales Theatre, London
Performed by the Martha Graham Dance Company

"I was quite pleased when Martha changed *Voyage* to *Circe.* It made a lot of sense. I thought it was a stroke of genius, but she has that kind of genius. Martha's genius, and the set, prevailed. You can even see that genius in her most recent dance, *Rite of Spring* (1984). That genius prevails.

"Martha was always redoing pieces. For instance, from *Circe* she took one thing and turned it into another, which is exactly what I had more or less perceived before she did the first *Voyage* (1953), which was a means to an end, the end having come with *Circe,* not with *Voyage.* One sometimes does something extemporaneously and it turns out to be something other than what one expected. Then one's instinct was better than one's thought. The thought process was faulty, but the instinct was O.K.

"It is still a voyage, with the tale of Ulysses, in *Circe.* It's the voyage—it's the rites of passage. It is even perfected in Joyce's *Ulysses.* We all go through phases. We even become animals. In the tale, everybody became a beast. It is the odyssey we all must take within ourselves. You see, it was with *Circe* that Martha specifically dealt with Ulysses. She had had Ulysses in mind for a very long time. She used to give me books on Ulysses. I'm like Ulysses, and Martha can transform people."

NOTES

Noguchi wrote, "Circe, the great enchantress, has turned all of Ulysses's companions into beasts. This is survival, stripped to essentials. The choreographic image is the curious mixing of people, set and space: submission to the image of desires. The sail, the boat are now in splendid harmony."

FROM THE ORIGINAL PROGRAM NOTES
"Whatever seeds each man cultivates will grow to
maturity and bear in him their own fruit. If
they be vegetative, he will be like a plant. If

sensitive, he will become brutish. If rational,
he will grow into a heavenly being. If in-
tellectual, he will be an angel, and the son of
God... Who would not admire this our chameleon?"
—Pico della Mirandola, 1486

"It was not fortune, but the desire of seeing the
world, that brought me here..."
—Ulysses to the Lion, from the Circe *of*
Giovanni Battista Gelli, *1549*

"The world Ulysses sees, in Martha Graham's adaptation of the myth of Circe, is his own: that inner world of bestialities and enchantments where one discovers what it costs to choose to be human."

© Nan Melville

© Nan Melville

CORTEGE OF EAGLES

Choreography by Martha Graham
Music by Eugene Lester
Set by Isamu Noguchi
Costumes by Martha Graham

Premiered February 21, 1967
Mark Hellinger Theater, New York
Performed by Martha Graham and Dance Company

"By the time of *Cortege of Eagles,* I wasn't making the core anymore because there was no more core. The core was Martha herself. I was making peripheral things. I used scrims and screens in *Cortege of Eagles,* but that is when I was getting to the end of my tether, so to speak. There was a misunderstanding. Martha was willing the dance into existence. I wasn't that taken with the dance. The creative thing was getting cluttered by the will, and contributions came from wishful thinking.

"They were not fixed sets, and then Martha wanted masks, but she couldn't [use them] because the dancers abhorred wearing them and refused to cover their faces in any way whatsoever. I don't know how in the world other people got dancers to wear masks. I made all these masks, but Martha couldn't use them because she had lost control over her company at the time. She was helpless."

NOTES

Noguchi wrote, " Based on the Hecuba *of Euripides, I wished to contrast the exquisite aristocratic rule of Troy destroyed by the rough dynamics of Greece, and likewise the dissolution and transformation of the noble queen (through the use of mask) into a mad dog. There were seven masks, and large kite-like forms moving into architectural and dynamic relationships. A sky floats in as well as, finally, the ghost of Hector. A significant invention was that of Charon the ferryman of the dead, as a master of ceremonies with a grotesque mask held between the teeth with one wild white eyeball and a lewd foot-long tongue."*

FROM THE ORIGINAL PROGRAM NOTES

"When Troy fell, Hecuba, its Queen, wife of Priam, could see wherever she turned the consequences of violence. Her son, Hector, the Trojan hero, had been killed by Achilles: Polyxena, her daughter, had been

*sacrificed on the tomb of Achilles; young Astyanax, the son of Hector and Andromache, had been sacri-
ficed to the God of War; Troy lay in ruins and untouched. Then Hecuba confronted the final inevitable
consequence of those times when violence prevails: she was driven to it herself.*

*"She and Priam had given their youngest son, Polydorus, into the safe-keeping of their friend, Polymnestor,
King of Thrace. Secretly, he murdered the boy, but Hecuba learned of it, and when, still feigning friendship,
he came to visit her in the ruins, she blinded him with her fingernails."*

© Johan Elbers

VARIABLE LANDSCAPE

Choreography by Kei Takei
Costumes by Kei Takei

First performed in May, 1978
Walker Arts Center, Minneapolis, Minnesota
Performed by Kei Takei's Moving Earth

This was a site-specific dance work created for performance in "Noguchi's Imaginary Landscape," a retrospective exhibition of Noguchi's sculptures curated by Martin Friedman.

Noguchi did not see this dance event.

JUDITH

Choreography by Martha Graham
Music by Edgar Varèse
Set by Isamu Noguchi
Costumes by Halston

Premiered April 29, 1980
Metropolitan Opera House, New York
Performed by the Martha Graham Dance Company

This was a re-working of the 1950 solo *Judith.* It became a company piece for the Martha Graham Dance Company and starred Peggy Lyman as Judith. The score by Edgard Varèse was used in lieu of William Schuman's original score.

FROM THE ORIGINAL PROGRAM NOTES
"The Assyrian came from the mountains of the North…
He threatened to set fire to my land,
Judith…disarmed him by the beauty of her face,
She put off her widow's weeds
To raise up the afflicted Israel;
She anointed her face with perfume,
And bound her hair with a headband,
And put on a linen gown to beguile him.
Her sandal entranced his eye,
Her beauty took his heart captive;
And the sword cut through his neck.
                                        —Judith"

Noguchi did not see this dance event.

PHAEDRA'S DREAM

Choreography by Martha Graham
Music by George Crumb
Set by Isamu Noguchi
Costumes by Halston

Premiered July 1, 1983
Herod Atticus Theatre, Athens, Greece
Performed by the Martha Graham Dance Company

The strong homosexual subplot, coupled with the fact that it premiered during the early stages of the AIDS epidemic in 1983, made this homoerotic dance even more controversial than *Phaedra*, which in 1962 had been deemed too pornographic to export on State Department-sponsored tours abroad. The action of *Phaedra* is precipitated by Phaedra's lie to Theseus that Hippolytus had sexually violated her. *Phaedra's Dream*, created in 1983, depicts the dream which precedes the action of the other dance. In fact, it is this dream which constitutes Phaedra's lie to Theseus. There are only three roles in *Phaedra's Dream*. Graham said in 1984, ". . . essentially of course, it's the attraction between man and mother and a man and a man. I'm very afraid of this piece. It's a little controversial. But Europe took it very well."[12]

FROM THE ORIGINAL PROGRAM NOTES
"Every woman at one moment in her life can foresee her prospects in a single gesture"—Marcel Proust

Noguchi did not see this dance event.

GOD'S ANGRY MEN, a passion play of John Brown

Choreography by Erick Hawkins

Music by Charles Mills, orchestrated by Lucia Dlugoszewski

Poetic text by Robert Richman

Set by Isamu Noguchi

Costume by Erick Hawkins

Revived October 17, 1984

Joyce Theatre, New York

Performed by the Erick Hawkins' Dance Company

See also John Brown, page 55.

This was a reworking of *John Brown* (1945). Erick Hawkins again played John Brown, the title role he had created nearly forty years earlier, in this production.

FROM THE ORIGINAL PROGRAM NOTES

"The composition of this dance was that of a young man, filled with dismay at the injustice in human society. It was performed at Constitution Hall in Washington, D.C., a month after the Daughters of the American Revolution denied the possibility of Marian Anderson's singing there because of her race. The premiere of this dance preceded the Civil Rights Act of 1964 by 19 years. The great problem of how to correct injustice is with us today almost as vividly as when John Brown decided to act. Perhaps the work is unique in its direct handling of an ethical issue in dance, with the collaboration of poetic text, music, and sculpture.

"Henry David Thoreau: 'John Brown's career for the last six weeks of his life was meteorlike, flashing through the darkness in which we live. I know of nothing so miraculous in our history.'

"Abraham Lincoln: 'John Brown's effort was peculiar. It was not a slave insurrection. It was an attempt by a white man to get up a revolt among slaves in which the slaves refused to participate. In fact, it was so absurd that the slaves, with all their ignorance, saw plainly enough it could not succeed.'

"Frederick Douglass: 'His zeal in the cause of my race was far greater than mine—it was the burning sun to my taper light—mine was bounded by time, his stretched away to the boundless shores of eternity.' "

Noguchi did not see this dance event.

NIGHT CHANT

Choreography by Martha Graham
Music by R. Carlos Nakai
Set by Isamu Noguchi
Costumes by Martha Graham and Halston

Premiered October 13, 1988
City Center, New York
Performed by the Martha Graham Dance Company

For the set of *Night Chant,* Graham turned around the Tree of Knowledge which Noguchi had created for *Embattled Garden* in 1958 and painted it black.

NOTES
Noguchi saw this dance. He said that it was fine that Martha Graham had reused the Tree of Knowledge, adding that "she is inventive in whatever she does." In addition, Noguchi told me that he had enjoyed taking a bow and receiving recognition at the performance. He died a little over two months later on December 30, 1988, in New York City.

1   Leon Theremin, inventor of the first electronic musical instrument, known as "Theremin rods," a console-like instrument capable of producing high tremolo effects. Theremin rods are featured prominently in Bernard Herrmann's score for *The Day the Earth Stood Still* and Miklos Rozsa used them to great effect in his 1945 Academy Award-winning score for Alfred Hitchcock's *Spellbound.* In addition, their eerie sounds can be heard in the opening of "Good Vibrations" by the Beach Boys.

2   Ruth Page, *Page by Page* (New York: Dance Horizons, 1978), p. 187.

3   "Frontier," a solo by Martha Graham, formed the first section of *Perspectives.* The second section, "Marching Song," was performed by Martha Graham and Group.

4   Page, *Page by Page*, p. 69.

5   "Turn O Libertad," from *Leaves of Grass.* Whitman's use of the Spanish word "Libertad" is generally taken as the personification of the concepts of liberty, freedom, privilege, immunity, and independence, or the person who enjoys them.

6   Robert Tracy, *Balanchine's Ballerinas: Conversations with the Muses* (New York: Simon & Schuster/Linden Press, 1983).

7   Review of Yuriko's concert October 23, 1949, at the Y.W.-Y.M.H.A., *Dance Observer*, 1949.

8   Izanagi-No-Mikoto and Izanami-No-Mikoto, the central gods of the Japanese creation myth, were the eighth pair of brother and sister gods to appear after the emergence of heaven and earth from chaos. Together they created many islands and deities. Izanami, fatally burned giving birth to the fire god, descends to the underworld where she partakes of its food, thereby preventing her from ever leaving. Izanagi goes to retrieve Izanami, but he is appalled by Izanami's appearance and escapes. He bathes to purify himself after coming in contact with the dead and as he bathes the sun goddess Amaterasu, the most important Shinto deity and from whom the Imperial family claimed descent, is born from his right eye, the moon god from his left eye, and the storm god from his nose.

9   Bertram Ross, interview by author, tape recording, New York, NY, 28 October 1996.

10   Bertram Ross interview, 28 October 1996.

11   This dance was denounced in Congress by Representatives Edna Kelley (R-NY) and Peter Freylinghuysen (R-NJ) as lewd. Since Graham received government money for State Department-sponsored tours abroad, the fact that the ballet was considered too erotic or "pornographic" to export caused a scandal.

12   *New York Daily News*, 26 February 1984.

EPILOGUE

"Isamu stopped working with me as he was more interested in gardens and playgrounds and pure monumental sculpture," said Martha Graham, in the late Sixties. "I've tried to woo him back into doing sets for me, but he isn't interested anymore."

Said Noguchi, "Well, I tried to do sculptures outside the stage, of course, without dancers, without actors, but at least it will stay there, and it is not dependent upon someone paying money to go and see the set and performance. The problem is in the selling of things and disposing of objects, of possessions. Outside the dance, the time limitations stay. For instance, when I do gardens or parks people can look at a garden or park in the same way they look at a dance only if they have the perspective to do so." Noguchi's public sculptures dating from the late Sixties include "Red Cube" (New York City), "Octetra" (Spoleto, Italy), and "Black Sun" (Seattle).

Noguchi, however, also felt that through destruction the possibility of creation exists. He believed in the possibility of rebuilding from destruction.

"It's always so," he said, "but you don't destroy yourself in the process. That is to say, what might help it? A form of destruction which is creative. It is not merely destruction. I say you can use bombs to make something, like I referred to in my 'This Tortured Earth' in 1943. The idea of sculpting the earth followed me through the years with mostly playground models as metaphors, but then there were others. 'This Tortured Earth' was my concept for a large area to memorialize the tragedy of war. There is injury to the earth itself. The war machine, I thought, would be excellent equipment for sculpture, to bomb it into existence. You can make a sculpture by bombing it from the air. It's a form of carving. But just to bomb is not the intention. It's not the intention to make sculpture with these guys who are dropping bombs all over the place. If they were told they had to do something with their feelings, with their landscape, well, they might very well become artists and stop dropping bombs."

Much of Noguchi's work consisted of public projects. He designed two bridges for the Peace Park at Hiroshima in 1952; from 1956-61, he created gardens for the Connecticut General Life Insurance Company which included 'The Family,' a large sculptural grouping. Of his 'Garden of Peace' (1956-58), created for the UNESCO building in Paris, Noguchi observed, "UNESCO was my beginning lesson in the use of stone."

Later he would say, "When I do break it [stone] and do this and that to it, in a way I'm making love to it. I'm really getting inside it. But I don't need to make shapes as many sculptors do. I try to dig into the fundamentals."

Noguchi's first plaza, for the First National City Bank in Ft. Worth, Texas, was executed in 1960-61. Between the years 1962-66, he created the Water Garden for Chase Manhattan Bank Plaza in New York City; the gardens for IBM and the Beinecke Library at Yale University; and the Billy Rose Art Garden in Jerusalem. In addition, his first playground, Kodomo-

No-Kumi, in Tokyo, was realized.

"I am always in an experimental mood," Noguchi remarked, "with trial and error. The dance is good training because it is never longer than two weeks in which I have to create a set. It doesn't get fouled up in pretentiousness." Noguchi, who could work on a single piece of stone for years, continued, "I like to work that way, in any case. It is part of me. As I said, it was a constant correlation of what I did in and out of the theater and my work. I never went too far away from what I was doing anyway.

"I think motivation can be one thing and end up quite differently," he observed. "Whatever motivates you is good, unless it's too sordid, like money. It gets you moving, because you are interested. As I said, mythology became Martha's language. What she did with it later is another matter. Other people couldn't use it very well because it became Martha. It restricted her eventually because she was tied into it. It was very painful for her to relinquish her roles to other people. She had to liberate herself again, which she did. It took some years.

"'Shock of recognition,' maybe that's it. There are certain elemental recollections that people recognize. I see this between Martha and me. We are all together in this curious world," Noguchi explained. "Absolutely. A dialogue with the audience is what Martha is having. I'm having a dialogue with the environment. Also, there is the idea of self-perception on the part of the viewing public. After all, unless there is a recognition on the part of the audience, you are beating your head against the wall. There are certain symbols that people react to. When people open up, take in, accept, assimilate, that's what a real dialogue is, and that's when a real dialogue begins. Martha has a very clever mind. She is erudite, and she knows what she is doing. It is not by accident that she creates, but by reading and assimilating knowledge. She is a very global woman. You are enriched. Martha in her use of my sets enriched the meaning. I may have suggested something, but she specifically puts it into experience. It is a new experience. It is also part of the sculptural experience.

"That is what I believe about sculpture anyway. It comes to life. I don't particularly like sculpture which is not in a sense adding to experience. That is the reason I'm changing all the time," he concluded. "You see, I think it is the artist's duty to use art in every way he can."

© Arnold Eagle

Photographic Acknowledgements
and Identification

Martha Graham, *Frontier,* 1935

1. Noguchi's mask of Michio Ito, 1926

2. Ruth Page, *Expanding Universe,* 1932

3. Martha Graham, *Frontier,* 1935

4. May O'Donnell, *Chronicle,* 1936

5. Pearl Lang and Rudolf Nureyev, *El Penitente,* 1975-76

6. Mikhail Baryshnikov, Pascal Rioualt, Joyce Herring, *El Penitente,* 1987

7. Wall and seat from *Herodiade,* similar to *Imagined Wing* design, 1944

8. Sculptural design, *Herodiade,* 1944

9. Martha Graham, *Herodiade,* 1944

10. Martha Graham, *Herodiade,* 1944

11. Martha Graham, *Herodiade,* 1944

12. Martha Graham, May O'Donnell, *Herodiade,* 1944

13. Martha Graham, *Herodiade,* 1950s

14. Martha Graham, Erick Hawkins, May O'Donnell, Yuriko, *Appalachian Spring,* 1944

15. Martha Graham, Erick Hawkins, May O'Donnell (seated), *Appalachian Spring,* 1944

16. Martha Graham, *Appalachian Spring,* 1944

17. Martha Graham, Erick Hawkins, May O'Donnell (seated), Merce Cunningham (kneeling), *Appalachian Spring,* 1944

18. Erick Hawkins, Martha Graham (seated), May O'Donnell (standing to Graham's right), *Appalachian Spring,* 1944

19. Martha Graham, Erick Hawkins, May O'Donnell, *Appalachian Spring,* 1944

20. Mikhail Baryshnikov, Rudolf Nureyev, Terese Capucilli, Maxine Sherman (seated), *Appalachian Spring,* 1987

21. Sculpture design for Erick Hawkins's, *John Brown,* 1945

22. Martha Graham and company, *Dark Meadow,* 1946

23. Martha Graham (on floor), May O'Donnell, Erick Hawkins, *Dark Meadow,* 1946

24. David Zellmer, Mark Ryder, Douglas Watson with Martha Graham, *Dark Meadow,* 1946

25. Martha Graham, Erick Hawkins, *Dark Meadow,* 1946

26. Martha Graham, Erick Hawkins, *Dark Meadow,* 1946

27. Ballet Russe, Frederick Franklin (center) *The Bells,* 1946

28. Alexandra Davilova, Frederick Franklin, Nikita Talin, *The Bells,* 1946

29. Martha Graham, Yuriko, Erick Hawkins, *Cave of the Heart,* 1947

30. Martha Graham, *Cave of the Heart,* 1947

31. Martha Graham, *Cave of the Heart,* 1947

32. Martha Graham, *Cave of the Heart,* 1947

33. Steve Rooks, Thea Nerissa Barnes, *Cave of the Heart,* 1984

34. Janet Elber, Yuriko Kimura, *Cave of the Heart,* 1979

35. Yuriko, *Shut Not Your Doors,* 1946

36. Erick Hawkins, Stuart Hodes, *Stephen Acrobat,* 1947

37. Sculptural design, *Errand Into the Maze,* 1947

38. Christine Dakin, *Errand Into the Maze,* 1947

39. Yuriko Kimura, *Errand Into the Maze,* 1979

40. Martha Graham, *Errand Into the Maze,* 1950's

41. Daniel Maloney, *Errand Into the Maze,* 1979

42. Helen McGehee and Clive Thompson, *Errand Into the Maze,* 1960s

43. Martha Graham, Erick Hawkins, *Night Journey,* 1947

44. Martha Graham, Bertram Ross, *Night Journey,* 1950s

45. Martha Graham, Bertram Ross, *Night Journey,* 1950s

46. Martha Graham, *Night Journey,* 1950s

47. Bertram Ross, Martha Graham, *Night Journey,* 1950s

48. Martha Graham, Bertram Ross, *Night Journey,* 1950s

49. Bertram Ross, Martha Graham, the daughters of the Night, *Night Journey,* 1950s

50. Martha Graham, Bertram Ross, *Night Journey,* 1950s

51. Martha Graham, *Night Journey,* 1950s

52. Martha Graham, *Night Journey,* 1947

53. Sculptural design, *The Seasons,* 1947

54. Yuriko, *Tale of Seizure,* 1948

55. Mikhail Baryshnikov, Kay Mezzo, *Orpheus,* 1979

56. George Balanchine, Mikhail Baryshnikov, *Orpheus,* 1979

57. Mikhail Baryshnikov, Christopher Fleming, Linda Homek, Nina Fedorova, *Orpheus,* 1979

58. Mikhail Baryshnikov, *Orpheus,* 1979

59. Peter Martins, *Orpheus,* 1979

60. Maria Tallchief, Nicholas Magallanes, *Orpheus,* 1948

61. Mikhail Baryshnikov, Kay Mezzo, *Orpheus,* 1979

62. Sculptural design, *Wilderness Stair,* 1948

63. Martha Graham, *Judith,* 1950

64. Martha Graham, *Judith,* 1950

65. Martha Graham, *Judith,* 1950

66. Martha Graham, *Judith,* 1950

67. Martha Graham, Bertram Ross, *Voyage,* 1953

68. Martha Graham, Bertram Ross, *Voyage,* 1953

69. Martha Graham, Bertram Ross, Stuart Hodes, Robert Cohan, *Theater of a Voyage,* 1955

70. Linda Hodes, Bertram Ross, Matt Turney, Helen McGehee, Mary Hinkson, *Seraphic Dialogue,* 1955

71. Mary Hinkson, Bertram Ross, Matt Turney, Helen McGehee, *Seraphic Dialolgue,* 1955

72. Martha Graham, *Clytemnestra,* 1958

73. Martha Graham, Bertram Ross and company, *Clytemnestra,* 1958

74. Martha Graham, Bertram Ross, *Clytemnestra,* 1958

75. Martha Graham, Paul Taylor, *Clytemnestra,* 1958

76. Martha Graham, Bertram Ross, *Clytemnestra,* 1958

77. Martha Graham, Bertram Ross and company, *Clytemnestra,* 1958

78. Martha Graham, *Clytemnestra,* 1958

79. Matt Turney, Paul Taylor, Mary Hinkson, Bertram Ross, *Embattled Garden,* 1958

80. Glen Tetley, Matt Turney, Yuriko, Bertram Ross, *Embattled Garden,* 1958

81. Matt Turney, Glen Tetley, Yuriko, Bertram Ross, *Embattled Garden,* 1958

82. Maxine Sherman, Lyndon Branaugh, *Embattled Garden,* 1984

83. Martha Graham, Dan Wagoner. Helen McGehee, *Acrobats of God,* 1960

84. Martha Graham, David Wood, Bertram Ross, Ethel Winter, *Acrobats of God,* 1960

85. Martha Graham, *Acrobats of God,* 1960

86. Martha Graham, *Acrobats of God,* 1960

87. Martha Graham, *Alcestis,* 1960

88. Martha Graham, Ethel Winter, Akiko Kando, Linda Hodes, *Alcestis,* 1960

89. Martha Graham, *Alcestis,* 1960

90. Martha Graham, Paul Taylor, Bertram Ross, *Alcestis,* 1960

91. Ken Topping, Christine Dakin, Denise Vale, *Phaedra,* 1988

92. Thea Nerissa Barnes, Ken Topping, *Phaedra,* 1988

93. Martha Graham, *Phaedra,* 1962

94. Mary Hinkson, Bertram Ross, *Circe,* 1963

95. Donlin Forman, Pascal Rioualt, Peter London, *Circe,* 1988

96. Donlin Forman, Pascal Rioualt, Peter London, *Circe,* 1988

97. Mary Hinkson, Clive Thompson, *Circe,* 1963

98. Peggy Lyman, Steve Rooks, *Cortege of Eagles,* 1984

99. Martha Graham (seated), Bertram Ross, Robert Cohen, *Cortege of Eagles,* 1969

100. Sculptural exhibit, Kei Takei's *Variable Landscape,* 1978

101. Peggy Lyman, George White Jr., *Judith,* 1980

102. George White Jr., *Phaedra's Dream,* 1984

103. Rudolf Nureyev, Christine Dakin, George White Jr., *Phaedra's Dream,* 1984

104. Terese Capucilli, Julian Littleford, *Phaedra's Dream,* 1984

105. Erick Hawkins, *God's Angry Men,* 1984

106. Denise Vale, George White Jr., *Night Chant,* 1988

107. Martha Graham, Isamu Noguchi, 1968-69

Photographic Acknowledgements

p. ii, 26-27, 29 © Barbara Morgan. Courtesty Willard and Barbara Morgan Archives, 45 Dorcester Avenue, Hastings-on-Hudson, New York 10706 (914) 478-0132. Lloyd and Douglas Morgan, Executors
p. 21, 23, 70, 71, 125, 193, 201, Courtesy Isamu Noguchi Foundation, Inc.

p. 31 © Louis Peres. Courtesy Louis Peres

p. 32-33, 52, 53, 72, 73, 85, 163, 178, 180-181, 186 (2), 199, 203 © Nan Melville. Courtesy Nan Melville.

p. 35, 39, 40, 41, 42, 45, 46, 47, 48, 49, 50, 51, 59, 60, 61, 94, 95, 96, 97, 98, 99, 100, 134, 135, 138-139, 142-143, 144, 150, 152-153, 154, 155, 156, 157, 160, 161, 162, 165, 166-167, 168, 169, 171, 172, 173, 174, 208, Noguchi Portrait © Arnold Eagle. Courtesy Mrs. Arnold Eagle on behalf of the Estate of Arnold Eagle.

p. 43, 128, 129, 130, 131 © Cris Alexander. Courtesy Cris Alexander.

p. 56 © David Fullard. Courtesy Isamu Noguchi Foundation, Inc.

p. 64 © Fred Fehl. Courtesy of Isamu Noguchi Foundation, Inc.

p. 65 Courtesy Jacobs Pillow Dance Festival, Lee, Masachusetts, Norton Owen, curator.

p. 69, 80, 93, 101 © Philippe Halsman Estate and Studio. Courtesy Stephen and Jane Halsman Bello.

p. 74, 87, 88, 89 © Max Waldman. Courtesy Carol Greunke, Executor, Max Waldman Archives.

p. 77, 109 Courtesy Yuriko

p. 84, 104-105 © Rudolf Burckhardt. Courtesy Rudolf Burckhardt

p. 86 Courtesy Lincoln Center Library and Museum of the Performing Arts, NYC. Curator Madeline Nichols and the staff of the Dance Collection.

p. 90 © Jaacov Agor. Courtesy Helen McGehee

p. 112-113, 114-115, 116, 117, 118, 120-121 © Carolyn George. Courtesy Carolyn George. *Orpheus* choreography by George Balanchine © The New York City Ballet. Balanchine is a trademark of the George Balanchine Trust.

p. 119 © George Platt Lynes. Courtesy Russell Lynes and the Dance Collection of the Library and Museum of the Performing Arts, NYC.

p. 151 © Sam Frank. Courtesy Bertram Ross.

p. 179 Martha Swope © Time Inc.

p. 184-185, 187 Anthony Crickmay © Theatre Museum, Victoria and Albert Museum, London. Courtesy Sarah Woodcock

p. 190, 198 © Johan Elbers. Courtesy Johan Elbers.

p. 191 © Fred Fehl. Courtesy Mrs. Fehl

p. 195 © Jack Vartoogian. Courtesy Jack Vartoogian.

p. 197 © Beatriz Shiller. Courtesy Beatriz Shiller.

Author's Acknowledgments

This book began when I created an independent study course, Martha Graham's Greek Cycle: A Survey of Graham's Interpretations Choreographically of Ancient Greek Drama, for my degree in Classical Studies from Skidmore College. My research for this project relied heavily on Graham's collaboration with the Japanese-American sculptor, Isamu Noguchi, and all of the sets he designed for her mythological productions. Six years later in 1983, I published my book on Balanchine's women, *Conversations with the Muses.* Since three of my major ballet teachers, Melissa Hayden, Maria Tallchief, and Violette Verdy, had all danced the role of Eurydice in the Stravinsky/Blanchine/Noguchi *Orpheus,* I decided to send Mr. Noguchi the book. He not only loved the book but invited me out to his recently opened museum in Long Island City, New York. He discovered that I had studied Greek and Latin and almost immediately we began documenting all of his 37 designs for the dance theater, a project that lasted for the next five years. Our last conversation was in the summer of 1988, when he invited me to a traditional Japanese lunch at his home and we conducted our final dialogue. We did speak by phone after he saw Graham's ballet, *Night Chant,* which incorporated Noguchi's Tree of Knowledge, and he suggested that I go see this new dance of Martha's, which I did. Soon after I moved to Paris and read in the *Herald Tribune* of his death on December 30, 1988.

Since I have been working on this book for 16 years, needless to say, I have a zillion people to thank. Here goes: I must begin with Mr. Noguchi and his phenomenal museum staff: Amy Hau, Museum Director; Soji Sadao, who had been with Mr. Noguchi forever; Alexandra Snyder, and curator Bonnie Rychlak. Then, first and foremost on my active team is Dorothy Eagle, who has allowed me access to all of the wonderful images photographed by her husband the late Arnold Eagle. I would also like to thank all of the other photographers for making their extraordinary work available to the public, my publisher, Mel Zerman, who has believed in me and this book for over ten years and his staff at Limelight Editions: Roxanna Font, Peter Cummins, most especially my designer, Bryan McHugh, and my copy-editor, Christine Dougherty, who sometimes knows my material better than I do because she has been working with me for so long.

Deserving a special mention are Joan Davidson Kaplan and Anne Birckmayer of the Furthermore Foundation, a division of The Publication Program of the J.M. Kaplan Fund, for demonstrating their belief in the importance of Noguchi as a major American sculptor by financially assisting in the publication of this book. I would like to thank all of my Skidmore connections including Isabel Brown, Jane Graves, Barbara Melville, Anne Palamountain, Mary Di Santo Rose and Kazuko Pettigrew.

My introduction to Martha Graham came through my teachers, Mary Hinkson, Ethel Winter and Lucinda Mitchell as well as through such acquaintances as Bertram Ross and John Wallowitch, May O'Donnell, Sophie Maslow, Jane Dudley, Bob Cohan, Matt Turney, Helen McGehee, Linda Hodes, David Wood and Marni Thomas, Yuriko, Pearl Lang, Donald McKayle, Paul Taylor, Merce Cunningham and the late John Cage, Glen Tetley, Takako Asakawa, Gus Solomons, Peggy Lyman, Elisa Monte and David Brown, Terese Capucilli, and to the late: Betty McDonald, Martha Hill, Anna Sokolow, Ray Green, Erick Hawkins, and Lucia Dlugoszewki, John Butler and Margot Fonteyn. Finally, I must thank Richard Move, Penny Frank, and Deborah Zoll who are also my Graham connections in the most positive way in terms of continuing Graham's astronomical legacy.

From the Balanchine organization I would like to thank Peter Martins and Darci Kistler, Barbara Morgan and the Balanchine Trust, Susan Hendl, Shaun O'Brien, Jacques D'Amboise, and Mikhail Baryshnikov. And I would like to also acknowledge the Rudolf Nureyev Dance Foundation, Barry Weinstein, Executor.

The artists who were instrumental in this stage design book include: Marisol, Robert Rauschenberg, Jasper Johns, Frank Stella, Bruce Nauman, Robert Morris, the late Andy Warhol, Alex Katz, Ellsworth Kelly, Robert Wilson, Frank Gehry, Jennifer Bartlett, the late Sol LeWitt, David Hockney, David Salle, Geoffrey Holder, Francesco Clemente, and the late Don Judd and Keith Haring. Thank you for continuing to design for the dance honoring the trajectories of both Noguchi and Diaghilev.

I would especially like to thank the professionals who have helped keep me in good health: Sue Graves and Ian Bjorklund, Dr. Eyhraune Jau-Saune, William Behr, Marius Morariu, Kent Helm, and Alan Good.

Finally, I would like to conclude by thanking the following friends and family: Hannie and Stanley Gillman, Sunny and Frederick DuPree, Samuel and Elizabeth Peabody, Christophe DeMenil, Mark Glick, the Kosugis, Juan Anduze, Alan and Paula Brody, Thomas DeFrantz and Christopher Pierce, Siobhan and Richard Dunham, Morris O'Connell and the National Museum of Dance, Mary Lou Whitney, Carolina and Reinaldo Herrera, Barbara Wright, Yannick, Yelena and Joakim Noah, Carol Judy Leslie, Yoko and Sean Ono Lennon, Janet Stapleton, the Shiva family, Jessye Norman, Phyllis and Jamie Wyeth, Martin Sherman, Lucinda Ramson, Carol and Earle Mack, Joe Marshall, Bill T. Jones, Bill Katz, Bijorn Amelan, Sarita Allen, Monona Wali, Wendy Richardson, Natalie Harley, Andréa Smith, Carlton Jones, Tania and Reza Badiyi, Tim Robbins, Chris Talbot, Ruben Carbajal, Susan Alexander, Dudley Williams, Alexandra Stewart and Justine Malle, Gelsey Kirkland and Greg Lawrence, Brooks Jackson, Mary Ellen Tracy, Ronald Perry, Ellen Jacobs, Odile Reine Adélaïde, Jodi Krizer, Rubinee Sathianathan and last but not least, through thick and thin, Chad Callis.

Robert Tracy was born in Boston and grew up in Milton, Massachusetts. He graduated from St. John's Preparatory School and earned his Bachelor of Arts Degree in Classical Studies and Dance from Skidmore College in Saratoga Springs, New York. At Skidmore he began his ballet training with New York City Ballet's Prima Ballerina Melissa Hayden, who had joined the college faculty as artist in residence upon her retirement from the stage. Simultaneously, he began his study of the Martha Graham modern dance technique with two of Graham's soloists, Mary Hinkson and Ethel Winter, and jazz dance at Alvin Ailey's.

Upon graduating from Skidmore, he performed for one year with Maria Tallchief's Chicago Lyric Opera Ballet before being awarded a three-year scholarship to George Balanchine and Lincoln Kirstein's School of American Ballet, where he appeared in Balanchine's recreation of "Le Bourgeois Gentilhomme" for Rudolf Nureyev and Patricia McBride and later in the same ballet with Suzanne Farrell and Peter Martins. Thereafter, he danced professionally most frequently in Nureyev's productions on Broadway and around the world.

As a journalist on dance, theater, music, art and film, Tracy has written for *The New York Times, Vanity Fair, Mademoiselle, Architectural Digest, Elle, Mirabella, Dance,* and the French, Spanish, German and English editions of *Vogue.* From 1989-1991, he wrote a monthly column for *Paris Vogue* about culture and fashion in New York City titled "New York en parle."

His first book, *Balanchine's Ballerinas: Conversations with the Muses,* published in 1983, was recognized by *The Wall Street Journal* as "this year's great ballet book." In 1986, he edited Nigel Gosling's *Prowling the Pavements: Selected Art Writings from London, 1950-1980.* Tracy researched and compiled Rudolf Nureyev's Introduction for Alexander Pushkin's, *The Golden Cockerel and Other Fairy Tales,* published in 1990. His dialogue, "Collaborating with Graham," was published in Isamu Noguchi's 1994 anthology, *Essays and Conversations.* His oral history *Goddess: Martha Graham's Dancers Remember* was published in 1997. In 1998 he wrote a commissioned entry on modern dancer Bill T. Jones for the *International Encyclopedia of Dance,* published by Oxford University Press. In the fall of 1999, he collaborated with Tim Robbins on the introduction to *Cradle Will Rock,* the companion book to the film Robbins directed. He wrote about 21 ballets performed by the Alvin Ailey American Dance Theater for their 1999-2000 Souvenir Program Book. In the spring of 2000, he wrote the panel essay on Alwin Nikolais for his induction into the Hall of Fame at the National Museum of Dance.

He received the Edward F. Albee Writing Fellowship in 1991 and the 1997 Skidmore College Alumni Association's Distinguished Achievement Award. In 1999 he was awarded a Furthermore Foundation Grant from the Kaplan Foundation.

Currently, he is at work on an oral history, *Hidden Rites: Alvin Ailey's Concert Dancers.* He lives in New York City.